"What's so great about economi
ter, we understand God better,
understand each other better. Bu
God intends for us to serve him—
According to Greg Forster, we a
every single moment of our lives. Your choices about where to eat or
toothbrush to buy may seem mundane, but Forster wants you to see them as
deeply profound. When you begin to see yourself in relation to the created
order, as Forster argues that you should, economics becomes no 'dismal science'; instead it becomes the most hopeful social science there is!"

    Victor V. Claar, BB&T Distinguished Professor of Free Enterprise
and Associate Professor of Economics, Florida Gulf Coast University;
coauthor, *Economics in Christian Perspective*

"Forster weaves together a masterful account of economic and intellectual
history with a deep understanding of the theological issues facing modern
Christians."

    P. J. Hill, Professor of Economics Emeritus, Wheaton College

"In this short book, Forster accomplishes what far larger economics books
fail to achieve, by laying out a theological, moral, and historical foundation
for economics. He leaves the technical details to others and instead gives his
readers an approachable introduction to human agency, cooperation, and
well-being, while also providing a tour through economic and intellectual
history. The result is a perfect complement to an economics or business
education, or an excellent guide to economics for those in the humanities. I
want all my students to read this book."

    Steven McMullen, Associate Professor of Economics, Hope College;
Executive Editor, *Faith & Economics*

"Each morning we wake up to an economic world, yet we often fail to grasp
the wonder, complexities, and challenges of modern free-market economies.
Few writers today are more intellectually robust and fairhanded, while also
engaging and accessible, than Greg Forster. Forster's deep grasp of theology as well as economics brings a rare and welcome historical perspective,
helping the reader grasp the rich contours of the past and wisely engage the
present realities of a free-market economy. Embracing a gospel centricity,
Forster rightly asserts that the gospel demands a new economic life and
paves the way for more virtuous economic exchange. Forster's book is a
treasure for all who desire a greater grasp of modern economic thought and
its integration with Christian theology. I highly recommend it."

    Tom Nelson, Senior Pastor, Christ Community Church, Kansas City;
President, Made to Flourish; author, *Work Matters* and *The Economics of
Neighborly Love*

"*Economics: A Student's Guide* introduces economics to undergraduates in a manner that is faithful to history and Christian theological commitments. Specialization, exchange, the role of money, competition, and economic growth are framed in the light of the scriptural values of justice and mercy. Students are invited into a consideration of how neighborly love is expressed in the marketplace through productive work, compassionate care for the poor, challenges to economic injustice, and encouragement of creativity. Current secular assumptions that incline us to blindly trust the market or political intervention are exposed, and in contrast, God's vision for restoration of economic harmony is explored. Any student wanting an introduction to how the distinctive wisdom of Scripture informs our view of the economy and the study of economics will surely benefit from this book."

Edd Noell, President, Association of Christian Economists; Professor of Economics and Business, Westmont College; coauthor, *Reckoning with Markets* and *Economic Growth*

~SERIES ENDORSEMENTS~

"Reclaiming the Christian Intellectual Tradition promises to be a very important series of guides—aimed at students—intended both to recover and instruct regarding the Christian intellectual tradition."

Robert B. Sloan, President, Houston Baptist University

"Reclaiming the Christian Intellectual Tradition is an exciting series that will freshly introduce readers to the riches of historic Christian thought and practice. As the modern secular academy struggles to reclaim a semblance of purpose, this series demonstrates why a deeply rooted Christian worldview offers an intellectual coherence so badly needed in our fragmented culture. Assembling a formidable cohort of respected evangelical scholars, the series promises to supply must-read orientations to the disciplines for the next generation of Christian students."

Thomas Kidd, Department of History, Baylor University

"This new series is exactly what Christian higher education needs to shore up its intellectual foundations for the challenges of the coming decades. Whether students are studying in professedly Christian institutions or in more traditionally secular settings, these volumes will provide a firm basis from which to withstand the dismissive attitude toward biblical thinking that seems so pervasive in the academy today. These titles will make their way onto the required reading lists for Christian colleges and universities seeking to ensure a firm biblical perspective for students, regardless of discipline. Similarly, campus pastors on secular campuses will find this series to be an invaluable bibliography for guiding students who are struggling with coalescing their emerging intellectual curiosity with their developing faith."

Carl E. Zylstra, President, Dordt College

ECONOMICS

ECONOMICS
A STUDENT'S GUIDE

Greg Forster

:: CROSSWAY®

WHEATON, ILLINOIS

Economics: A Student's Guide

Copyright © 2019 by Greg Forster

Published by Crossway
        1300 Crescent Street
        Wheaton, Illinois 60187

Cover design: Jon McGrath, Simplicated Studio

First printing, 2019

Printed in the United States of America

Scripture quotations are from the ESV® Bible (The Holy Bible, English Standard Version®), copyright © 2001 by Crossway, a publishing ministry of Good News Publishers. Used by permission. All rights reserved.

Trade paperback ISBN: 978-1-4335-3923-7
ePub ISBN: 978-1-4335-3926-8
PDF ISBN: 978-1-4335-3924-4
Mobipocket ISBN: 978-1-4335-3925-1

Library of Congress Cataloging-in-Publication Data

Names: Forster, Greg, 1973– author.
Title: Economics: a student's guide / Greg Forster.
Description: Wheaton: Crossway, 2019. | Series: Reclaiming the Christian intellectual tradition | Includes bibliographical references and index.
Identifiers: LCCN 2019005975 (print) | LCCN 2019021800 (ebook) | ISBN 9781433539244 (pdf) | ISBN 9781433539251 (mobi) | ISBN 9781433539268 (epub) | ISBN 9781433539237 (tp)
Subjects: LCSH: Economics—Religious aspects—Christianity.
Classification: LCC BR115.E3 (ebook) | LCC BR115.E3 F67 2019 (print) | DDC 261.8/5—dc23
LC record available at https://lccn.loc.gov/2019005975

Crossway is a publishing ministry of Good News Publishers.

CH		27	26	25	24	23	22	21	20	19
14	13	12	11	10	9	8	7	6	5	4	3	2	1

This book is dedicated to

P. J. Hill, Victor Claar, and Brian Fikkert,

for doing so much to help me
understand their discipline,

and for their leadership in helping their
discipline think with the mind of Christ.

In that night God appeared to Solomon, and said to him, "Ask what I shall give you." And Solomon said to God, "You have shown great and steadfast love to David my father, and have made me king in his place. O LORD God, let your word to David my father be now fulfilled, for you have made me king over a people as numerous as the dust of the earth. Give me now wisdom and knowledge to go out and come in before this people, for who can govern this people of yours, which is so great?" God answered Solomon, "Because this was in your heart, and you have not asked for possessions, wealth, honor, or the life of those who hate you, and have not even asked for long life, but have asked for wisdom and knowledge for yourself that you may govern my people over whom I have made you king, wisdom and knowledge are granted to you. I will also give you riches, possessions, and honor, such as none of the kings had who were before you, and none after you shall have the like."

2 Chronicles 1:7–12

CONTENTS

Series Preface   11

1   The Economy: How We Steward the World Together   15

2   Justice and Mercy: Key Scriptural Teachings for Economic
Arrangements   35

3   The Ancient Crisis: From Natural to Supernatural Economics   53

4   The Medieval Crisis: From Conventional to Reforming
Economics   67

5   The Modern Crisis: From Static to Dynamic Economics   83

6   Economic Idols and Economic Wisdom: From Ideological
Captivity to Theological Transformation   99

Questions for Reflection   113

Glossary   115

Resources for Further Study   117

General Index   119

Scripture Index   125

SERIES PREFACE

RECLAIMING THE CHRISTIAN INTELLECTUAL TRADITION

The Reclaiming the Christian Intellectual Tradition series is designed to provide an overview of the distinctive way the church has read the Bible, formulated doctrine, provided education, and engaged the culture. The contributors to this series all agree that personal faith and genuine Christian piety are essential for the life of Christ followers and for the church. These contributors also believe that helping others recognize the importance of serious thinking about God, Scripture, and the world needs a renewed emphasis at this time in order that the truth claims of the Christian faith can be passed along from one generation to the next. The study guides in this series will enable us to see afresh how the Christian faith shapes how we live, how we think, how we write books, how we govern society, and how we relate to one another in our churches and social structures. The richness of the Christian intellectual tradition provides guidance for the complex challenges that believers face in this world.

This series is particularly designed for Christian students and others associated with college and university campuses, including faculty, staff, trustees, and other various constituents. The contributors to the series will explore how the Bible has been interpreted in the history of the church, as well as how theology has been formulated. They will ask: How does the Christian faith influence our understanding of culture, literature, philosophy, government, beauty, art, or work? How does the Christian intellectual tradition help us understand truth? How does the Christian intellectual tradition shape our approach to education? We believe that this series is not only timely but that it meets an important need, because the secular culture in which we now find ourselves is, at best, indifferent to the Christian faith, and the Christian world—at least in its more popular forms—tends to be confused about the beliefs, heritage, and tradition associated with the Christian faith.

At the heart of this work is the challenge to prepare a generation of Christians to think Christianly, to engage the academy and the culture, and to serve church and society. We believe that both the breadth and the depth of the Christian intellectual tradition need to be reclaimed, revitalized, renewed, and revived for us to carry this work forward. These study guides will seek to provide a framework to help introduce students to the great tradition of Christian thinking, seeking to highlight its importance for understanding the world, its significance for serving both church and society, and its application for Christian thinking and learning. The series is a starting point for exploring important ideas and issues such as truth, meaning, beauty, and justice.

We trust that the series will help introduce readers to the apostles, church fathers, Reformers, philosophers, theologians, historians, and a wide variety of other significant thinkers. In addition to well-known leaders such as Clement, Origen, Augustine, Thomas Aquinas, Martin Luther, and Jonathan Edwards, readers will be pointed to William Wilberforce, G. K. Chesterton, T. S. Eliot, Dorothy Sayers, C. S. Lewis, Johann Sebastian Bach, Isaac Newton, Johannes Kepler, George Washington Carver, Elizabeth Fox-Genovese, Michael Polanyi, Henry Luke Orombi, and many others. In doing so, we hope to introduce those who throughout history have demonstrated that it is indeed possible to be serious about the life of the mind while simultaneously being deeply committed Christians.

These efforts to strengthen serious Christian thinking and scholarship will not be limited to the study of theology, scriptural interpretation, or philosophy, even though these areas provide the framework for understanding the Christian faith for all other areas of exploration. In order for us to reclaim and advance the Christian intellectual tradition, we must have some understanding of the tradition itself. The volumes in this series seek to explore this tradition and its application for our twenty-first-century world. Each volume contains study questions, a glossary, and a list of resources for further study, which we trust will provide helpful guidance for our readers.

I am deeply grateful to the series editorial committee: Timothy George, John Woodbridge, Michael Wilkins, Niel Nielson, Philip Ryken, and Hunter Baker. Each of these colleagues joins me in thanking our various contributors for their fine work. We all express our appreciation to Justin Taylor, Jill Carter, Allan Fisher, Lane Dennis, and the Crossway team for their enthusiastic support for the project. We offer the project with the hope that students will be helped, faculty and Christian leaders will be encouraged, institutions will be strengthened, churches will be built up, and, ultimately, that God will be glorified.

Soli Deo Gloria
David S. Dockery
Series Editor

1

THE ECONOMY

HOW WE STEWARD THE WORLD TOGETHER

Everywhere you go, people care passionately about the economic side of life. At the personal level, worrying about job security has become the new normal for millions of people of every socioeconomic level, and money trouble is one of the key factors in every kind of personal calamity, from divorce to addiction. At the organizational level, we all do our daily work as part of organizations that have a bottom line and have to "make payroll" every week to survive. (This includes colleges, churches, other nonprofits, and even government entities, as well as businesses!) At the social level, there is never a moment when our public life is not dominated by debates over economic policy. Intergenerational poverty remains one of our most weighty challenges. And the future of our civilization seems to depend on whether we can figure out the right response to the unprecedented developments of technological progress and globalization. All our social systems were designed for a world in which muscle power was highly valued and nations were mostly separate from one another. Drastically increased mechanization of physical labor and the movement of goods, people, and communication across boundaries and enormous distances is now confronting us with challenges our systems weren't built to face.

Looking at all those challenges, it's no wonder economists joke that their field is "the dismal science." But it is possible to see these things from another perspective. The Christian intellectual tradition, building on the revelation of God in Christ by the Spirit in the word, has spent two thousand years helping people lift their eyes to a higher reality that lies behind these troubling experiences.

THE GOSPEL IN A WORLD OF ECONOMIC TROUBLES

We live in a world of troubles, many of which are economic. But why do we live in such a world? That is a theological question— in fact, it is one of the oldest theological questions, as the book of Job reminds us. If our experience of economics, like our experience of everything else, is dominated by the dismal, it seems only natural to ask why the dismal dominates. If theology has an answer to that question, as Christians believe it does, then it could help us look at our economic world in a whole new way.

What if our daily struggles to keep a job and make ends meet, our organizational struggles to make payroll and keep the lights on, and our societal struggles to manage public economic concerns are really battles in a cosmic civil war between God and Satan? What if every time we allow our economic actions to pursue greed, sloth, pride, envy, gluttony, lust, and wrath, we are surrendering a hill, a bridge, or an airstrip to the armies of our eternal enemy? What if every time we manage our economic affairs—from the personal to the public—with the justice and mercy of our gracious and powerful God, we are striking back against our ghostly foe and reclaiming a little piece of the world for the holy love of God? How can Christians develop ways of thinking about and participating in the economy that take it seriously as a major strategic front in the holy war between God and Satan for the fate of the universe?

Why, no, as a matter of fact, this is not an ordinary economics textbook.

This is a book about economics, not a book of theology as such. Our focus is economic affairs, from balancing checkbooks to globalization, poverty, growth, and debt. But we will be looking at the economy through the lens of the Christian intellectual tradition, seeing these things as the church has seen them in the light of Scripture and the Spirit.

This chapter provides an overview of how the economic side of life can be understood as part of a Christian worldview. Chapter 2 turns to Scripture and reviews key elements of the testimony of God's Word on economic matters. These are the foundations on which the Christian intellectual tradition has built a theological view of the economy.

Of course it's true that Augustine never wrote about global markets, Thomas Aquinas never commented on industrialization, and Martin Luther had nothing to say about digital finance, for the very good reason that these things did not exist when they lived. But as we will see in chapter 3, Augustine and his ancient contemporaries did describe how the gospel compels us to see economic affairs in a dramatically different way. As we will see in chapter 4, Aquinas and his medieval contemporaries did describe how this new worldview could be worked out in economic systems and behaviors on both large and small scales. And as we will see in chapter 5, Luther and his early modern contemporaries did describe how the economic reforms brought into the world by Christianity were leading in radically unexpected directions, with the potential to reshape the world. Only by recovering a theological view of economics, which the Christian intellectual tradition provides, can we hope to think faithfully about our own economic challenges.

However, we face a challenge they did not face—and I'm not talking about globalization. I'm talking about a more subtle challenge. Our way of life and our categories of thought have become separated from the Christian intellectual tradition. There were many historical differences between Augustine in the fifth century and Luther in the sixteenth, but for all that, they did share a lot of common ground in the way they thought about the world. That vast area of common ground has become, for us, a lost continent. As we will see in chapter 6, the economic thought of the modern world has become detached from Christian thought and is deeply shaped by various secular and pagan ways of understanding the world. Christians today are, in general, not much aware of how deeply we have allowed these secular and pagan assumptions to shape our views and behaviors. As a result, it is much harder for us than it was for our spiritual ancestors to view economics in a Christian way. In chapter 6, we will look at some starting points for reforming our economic thinking and acting.

THE ECONOMY IN A BROAD SENSE: MAKING CHOICES ABOUT RESOURCES

"The economy" and "economics" are not the same thing. It's easy to say what economics is: it's the academic discipline that studies the economy, just as political science is the discipline that studies politics and chemistry is the discipline that studies chemicals. When people say they want a Christian view of economics, usually what they really mean is that they want a Christian view of the economy. It certainly wouldn't do much good to develop a Christian view of political science without developing a Christian view of politics!

But what is the economy? That, it turns out, is a harder question.

When people hear the term "the economy," they usually get two images in their minds. One is confusing graphs, bewildering mathematical formulas, and endless spreadsheets of numbers. The other is talking heads on a screen, yelling at each other about public policy.

Those things are not the economy. They are the two main ways our advanced modern world *talks about* the economy. And they do have important roles. Graphs, formulas, and spreadsheets make it possible for us to manage large amounts of economic information. Take a course on economics or just read one of those ordinary economics textbooks, and the graphs and charts will be much less bewildering. Likewise, every society needs to have public-policy debates. Our government is going to make economic policy one way or another; if we didn't have public debates about it, the policymakers would just do their work secretly, unaccountable for the way they used their power. (Granted, the "yelling at each other" part is something we could do without.)

To understand the economy, however, we have to go behind the graphs and the debaters. We have to see the things they're describing and arguing about.

So what is the economy? Let's begin with what academic economists say. For the field of economics, the standard definition of the economy focuses on the choices people make about using resources.

Specifically, by the standard definition, the economy is how we make decisions about using resources that are limited in amount or availability.[1] Economists call these "scarce" resources, but they're using the term *scarce* in a special, technical sense. Imagine a gigantic warehouse full of thousands of crates of 12-ounce soda cans. In that warehouse, soda is not "scarce" in the way we usually mean, because it is very abundant. There's a lot of it. But soda is still "scarce" in the way economists mean, because it is still limited. The amount of soda in the warehouse is not infinite; if you start putting it on trucks and shipping it to grocery stores, eventually you will run out.

This means the economy is largely about trade-offs. Because most resources are limited in some way, our decisions about how to use them involve trading off one possible use for another. If I have a limited supply of food in my refrigerator, any choice I make to use that food in one way (such as eating it) reduces my opportunity to use it in other ways (letting others in my household eat it, bringing it to a church luncheon, or gluing it to the wall to make avant-garde

---

[1] See Victor V. Claar and Robin J. Klay, *Economics in Christian Perspective: Theory, Policy, and Life Choices* (Downers Grove, IL: InterVarsity Press, 2007), 15–16, 26–34.

artwork). I can certainly choose to eat some of the food, give some to my family, bring some to church, and glue some to the wall. But each item of food I use in one way is an item I can't use in another way. By contrast, my supply of air is effectively unlimited, so the choices I make about how to use air do not involve those kinds of trade-offs. That is why the choices I make about food are economic choices, while the choices I make about air are not.

This leads us to a very important insight: the economy is not just about money. Money is very important, but it is only one kind of economic resource. There are millions of economic resources. If we are thinking only about money, we are not thinking about the economy; we are thinking about one important but limited *part* of the economy. And the money part of the economy does not somehow control all the rest and render it irrelevant. On the contrary, many of the decisions you make about how to use your money are driven by decisions you've made about other economic resources and opportunities—you don't go to college because it gives you an excuse to take out that student loan you've always dreamed of having; you take out the loan because you want to go to college.

To see why the economy is so much more than money, it helps to consider three of the major categories of economic resources recognized by academic economists.[2] One category is money and material goods—houses, cars, phones, breakfast cereal, video games, coffee, and all those sorts of things. A second category is time. You have a limited amount of time, and at every moment you are making choices about how to use your time that involve economic trade-offs. An economist friend of mine says time is his favorite economic resource because it's the great equalizer—it's the only thing we all have the same amount of. You can spend money to hire other people to use their time doing things for you, but you cannot increase or decrease the number of hours you have each day. A third category is reputation. We can see how reputation is

---

[2] See Claar and Klay, *Economics*, 26–34.

an economic resource most easily when, for example, a celebrity takes money to endorse a product. But that's just the tip of the iceberg. All of us are constantly thinking about how other people see us, and adjusting our behavior accordingly. All day long, we are managing our reputations as a limited resource. We often spend large amounts of money and time to do things that we hope will improve the way others see us. This also goes the other way, because we "spend" or "invest" reputation whenever we endorse or argue in favor of something, such as when you tell your skeptical friend that a certain book or movie is worth his or her time.

THE ECONOMY IN A NARROWER SENSE: SYSTEMS OF EXCHANGE AND SPECIALIZATION

The economy is not just money. It's the complex system of choices we make about all our resources (including money), all our time, and all our standing in the eyes of others. Every choice we make throughout the day that involves managing these resources is an economic choice.

And let's face it, that's pretty much all our choices, at some level! There is no area of life that is not economic in at least some way. Even prayer involves economic decisions, because you are making a choice about how you use your time. You might even be making the wrong choice! As C. S. Lewis said, in the middle of a prayer "you may realize that, instead of saying your prayers, you ought to be downstairs . . . helping your wife to wash up. Well, go and do it."[3] The scriptural injunction to "pray without ceasing" (1 Thess. 5:17) means we should do everything in a prayerful way, not that we should stop working (Ex. 20:9), resting (Ps. 127:2), and enjoying life (1 Tim. 6:17) in order to do nothing but pray. That means making economic decisions about when to pray and when to work, rest, enjoy, and so forth.

---

[3] C. S. Lewis, *Mere Christianity*, in The Complete C. S. Lewis Signature Classics (New York: Harper-One, 2002), 102.

The economy is not all there is to life, however. We wouldn't want to reduce everything to merely economic concerns and nothing else. The everyday life of a marriage or a church involves making economic decisions, but they are not economic institutions at their core. Faithfulness to a spouse or to God cannot be reduced merely to how we manage resources.

To avoid the danger of thinking that the economy is literally everything, let's look at a narrower way we can define the economy. When we talk about "the economy," we usually mean the special activities and institutions that exist specifically to help us manage economic decisions.

Here it is useful to look at two key concepts from academic economics: exchange and specialization. *Exchange* simply means buying, selling, or trading. *Specialization* means focusing the use of your resources on fewer things—typically on the activities in which you get the biggest "bang for the buck," in which you can produce the most beneficial results from a given investment of resources.

You and I both need shirts and shoes. I could make my own shirts and shoes, and you could make your own shirts and shoes. But if I'm a better shoemaker and a worse shirt-maker than you, while you're a better shirt-maker and a worse shoemaker than me, we'll both be a lot better off if I spend my hours making shoes and you spend your hours making shirts. Then we can trade, your shirts for my shoes.

Money is a tool that allows us to make these exchanges more efficiently. Instead of trading goods for goods, which is inconvenient and imprecise, we can buy and sell. I make shoes and sell them, and use the money to buy your shirts; you make shirts and sell them, and use the money to buy my shoes.

People have widely varying talents and interests, and that means we are all better at some things than others. Most of us have only a few things that we can do well enough that it makes sense for us to invest lots of time in them. When people have to manage limited resources—including limited time!—they figure out pretty quickly that they can get more done by specializing in the things they do best, then exchanging with others to take care of the things they don't specialize in. This principle was recognized as far back as Plato in ancient Greece, and it has been the central pillar of the study of economics ever since.[4]

What we call "the economy" is millions of people around the world trading their work with one another. When we do our jobs, we are specializing—devoting our work hours to doing one kind of work. When we buy and sell, we are meeting our needs and desires by exchanging with others who, in their jobs, are specializing in the kinds of work we need. We can sum up "the economy" as the vast system of exchange that helps us all use our resources more efficiently than we could on our own. Each of us, as an individual, makes use of the world. The world provides us with material objects (goods), opportunities for different kinds of activities (time), and relationships with others (reputation). We each use what the world provides. The economy allows us to exchange with others so we can make better, or at least more efficient, use of the world.

Here's another important principle: the more different people we exchange with, the more benefits we get from specializing and exchanging. Everyone is better off when there is a greater variety of options for how to distribute tasks across the population. A village that lives in total isolation will typically have some specialization—there might be one person who is a full-time carpenter, another who is a full-time religious leader, and so forth—but most of the people in that village will have to be farmers. There's just no other option; the food has to come from somewhere. But suppose we have a kingdom with fifty such villages, and the king builds new roads that allow all these villages to start trading with one another. The thirty villages that have the biggest agricultural advantages—

---

[4] In Plato's *Republic*, Socrates describes the principle of specialization, or division of labor, more or less as economists hold it to this day. See Plato, *The Republic of Plato* (New York: Basic Books, 1991), 47 (370b–370c).

maybe they're located on the best land or beside rivers with lots of fish—could specialize in food production, and the other twenty villages could drastically cut back food production and make other things to sell for food: handicrafts, improved tools, art, religious goods—you name it. There would be an explosion of economic production. Now suppose the king concludes a peace treaty that allows this kingdom to start trading with ten other kingdoms like it. The whole kingdom—all fifty villages—might suddenly find that they can pull back food production and start working on developing new technologies, schools of philosophy and literature, religious orders, or any number of things. Or they might find that they're the top food producers in the region and go back to farming so others can do other things!

This is the whole reason globalization is such a chaotic whirlwind. For the first time in history, new technologies and accompanying political developments (especially the defeat of the fascist and communist powers) are making it possible for almost everyone in the whole world to trade. This has produced an explosion of economic growth. Every region of the world is now growing, and poverty rates are plummeting worldwide. From 1970 to 2006, the number of people living on a dollar per day or less fell by 80 percent, while living standards more than doubled.[5]

More important than the material benefits of global markets, however, are the moral benefits. Economic development and access to global markets are interdependent with political liberation, democratic self-government, equal dignity for women, religious freedom, and other essential moral goods. Around the world, the freedom to trade and build is linked with the freedom to think, speak, and act with human dignity. Even highly oppressive, authoritarian regimes are often forced to moderate their brutality so as not to disrupt their access to global markets. The governments

---

[5] Maxim Pinkovskiy and Xavier Sala-i-Martin, "Parametric Estimations of the World Distribution of Income," National Bureau of Economic Research, October 2009; other estimates yield different numbers, but all estimates agree there was a very large global decline in extreme poverty.

of Russia and China, which systematically murdered about 100 million of their own people with total impunity in the twentieth century, cannot now indulge even in bellicose rhetoric without first at least considering how financial markets and trade partners will respond. Of course, they often use bribes or threats to get around the constraints of the global marketplace. But that is a big step up from the way things were before globalization, when their murderous tyranny faced few constraints short of open war.

At the same time, globalization's explosion of opportunities for exchange is bringing drastic changes in what kind of specialization—the distribution of tasks among populations—makes sense. People who used to have a secure living doing specific kinds of work find that it's no longer profitable to do those kinds of work in their countries. So the enormous economic growth of globalization, which every region of the world is benefiting from, is upsetting long-standing social arrangements in every one of those regions. It remains to be seen how our political and social systems will respond to such sweeping economic change; they were not built with this kind of drastic transformation in mind. But there's no going back, unless you can uninvent computers, satellites, jetliners, and shipping containers—or want to place your hope in oppressive political movements that arbitrarily cut off people's access to markets, or bring back global military confrontations that paralyze trade.

WITHOUT GOD—*HOMO ECONOMICUS*

Disruption of long-settled ways of life is not the only problem created by the enormous power of modern market systems. A more subtle but equally serious problem is the tendency to reduce people to mere economic units. The power of economic exchange is so overwhelming that societies begin to treat people as if participating in economic exchange is their highest purpose.

As historic religious commitments have lost influence in the public square, deep spiritual perspectives on human life have faded.

More materialistic views of humanity, in which people have no supernatural purpose, have grown influential. The two dominant paradigms for understanding human life in this secular context are economics and sexuality. People increasingly treat one another as merely biological animals whose lives are dominated by animal concerns: immediate gratification of sexual urges and the accumulation of material resources to keep our bellies fed.

The issue is a culture's underlying anthropology, our understanding of what it means to be human. In the nineteenth and twentieth centuries, academic economists developed a materialistic anthropology that allowed them to study economic behavior without taking account of moral and spiritual realities. This model has sometimes been called *homo economicus*. Brian Fikkert and Michael Rhodes have summed up *homo economicus* as the view that God is irrelevant to happiness, that people have autonomous (self-generated) consumption-oriented desires and become happy by satisfying those desires, that the world exists to provide raw material for these autonomous consumption desires, and that people are naturally in a state of rivalry with one another because their autonomous consumption desires conflict.[6]

This materialistic view of life has gradually extended beyond academic economics to dominate our daily lives in many ways. In our workplaces and marketplaces, we are culturally formed by structures built on the assumption that human beings are essentially consumers who will become happy when they satisfy their autonomous consumption desires. This has happened partly because our cultures, having become disconnected from their historic religious narratives, needed some sort of explanatory structure to tell them how to arrange the new global economy, and *homo economicus* was a readily available narrative. And it has happened partly because the narratives of academic economics became so-

---

[6]Brian Fikkert and Michael Rhodes, "*Homo Economicus* Versus *Homo Imago Dei*," *Journal of Markets & Morality* 20, no. 1 (Spring 2017): 101–26.

cially influential through large institutions staffed by economists trained in the academy, where *homo economicus* is the dominant anthropology.

The emptiness of life on the *homo economicus* model is increasingly clear to increasingly large numbers of people. The question is, Where will our cultures turn for an alternative explanation of the moral significance of economic relationships and their rightful place in the grand scheme of human life?

WHAT IS THE ECONOMY?
A THEOLOGICAL PERSPECTIVE

The academic discipline of economics says the economy is how people exchange with others to use the world more efficiently. Scripture and the Christian intellectual tradition do not contradict this. But they do force us to rethink what it means. Here, as everywhere else, theology does not simply toss out everything believers know from our natural sources of knowledge and replace it. Rather, Scripture corrects and perfects our natural knowledge.

According to Scripture, human beings were made to be good stewards of God's world. In Genesis 1, the statement that Adam and Eve were made in the "image of God" is closely associated with their position as stewards of God's world. Word choices in the Hebrew text indicate God made Adam and Eve in his image *so that* they would be fruitful and multiply, have dominion, fill the earth, and subdue it.[7] Genesis 2:15 says that God placed Adam in the garden "to work it and keep it." This calling to be good stewards of the world continues throughout Scripture and is central to the biblical conception of God's intention for human life.[8]

A steward is someone who has the authority to manage something on behalf of its owner. In the ancient world, the head of a large household would appoint stewards to oversee household

---

[7] See J. Michael Thigpen, "Creation and Economics," Oikonomia Network, https://oikonomia network.org/resources/creation-and-economics.
[8] See *NIV Stewardship Study Bible* (Grand Rapids, MI: Zondervan, 2009).

business. Human beings have been given authority over God's world to manage it for God.

The two key concepts of stewardship in Genesis are cultivating and protecting; this is the meaning of the Hebrew words translated as "work" and "keep" in Genesis 2:15.[9] Cultivating is central because God made a world full of potential, and he made us to do work that transforms the world to bring out its potential. For example, all the materials that make up a smartphone—mostly sand—were in the world from the beginning. What is the difference between sand and a smartphone? Lots of human work, ingenuity, and exchange. That's the image of God. Protecting the world is central because God made the world to manifest his qualities to us—his beauty, power, holiness, love, and so on. If we don't take good care of the world, God's beautiful creation will be squandered and abused.

Why does God want stewards for his world? Because stewardship is the primary way people enjoy the holy love of God and manifest it within his creation. We bring God's holy love into his world by managing it with the spiritual power that God's love gives us. God created us because he is three persons who love each other in perfect holiness and blessedness, and God wants to share that love with more people. And love is a two-way street. We receive God's love, but we also love God in return. We do so by putting his holy love into action in the way we live. That primarily means being good stewards of the world he gave us.

You may want to object that the main way people love God is by worshiping him. But the concept of worship in the Bible does not just include what we do on Sunday morning or when we engage in other special religious activities. Worship includes everything we do that exercises the holy love of God. When you write a report, drive a truck, sweep a floor, or change a diaper as an act of Chris-

---

[9] Seong Hyun Park, "Working and Keeping," Oikonomia Network newsletter, February 20, 2014, https://oikonomianetwork.org/2014/02/working-and-keeping/.

tian love for God and neighbor, that is worship. All good stewardship is worship.[10]

But people were not made to steward the world alone. The
possibility that Adam might exercise his stewardship alone in the
world is the only thing that is called "not good" in the creation account (Gen. 2:18). God doesn't make Eve solely for reproduction
or to give Adam someone to talk to. God says that he is making
Eve as a "helper" to cooperate with Adam in the job of humanity—exercising stewardship over the world.

Human beings are relational creatures. We are never isolated
individuals. We do have individual hearts, minds, and wills, and that
is why every individual matters. But our individual hearts, minds,
and wills never exist in isolation from the hearts, minds, and wills
of other people. Who we are as human beings is defined by our relationships with God, with one another, with the natural world, and
even with ourselves (in our sense of identity and purpose).

Just as God himself is three persons who love each other and
always work together, God has made human beings in his image
to work together as his stewards. We were made to steward the
world *together*. And that is where a Christian view of the economy
comes in.

The economy is how we use the world. The biblical concept of
stewardship provides a standard against which the way people use
the world can be judged. In theory, economists claim that they only
describe how people use resources; they supposedly don't make any
assumptions about how people ought to use those resources. In
practice, however, nobody ever describes anything without making
assumptions about how the world is supposed to work. As a witty
Christian economist once put it, we typically measure the size of
an economy in terms of gross domestic production per person,
but not gross domestic production per rabbit, so we are assuming

---

[10] See Tom Nelson, *Work Matters: Connecting Sunday Worship to Monday Work* (Wheaton, IL: Crossway, 2011).

people matter in a way rabbits do not. The discipline of economics is shot through with assumptions about what is good and bad; for example, economists assume that growth is good and poverty is bad. But how can people evaluate assumptions about what is economically good and bad? The Christian claim that we were made to steward the world for God, and thus bring the holy love of God into his world, gives us a standard.

The economy also involves how people specialize and exchange to use the world more efficiently. The biblical concept that human beings are relational creatures, made to steward the world together, provides a standard for what their economic specialization and exchange ought to look like. Once again, in theory, economists are supposed to merely describe how people specialize and exchange; they're not supposed to make assumptions about how that specialization and exchange should be carried out. In practice, however, they do so all the time. Economists are constantly giving their opinions about public policy—taxes, regulation, trade, contract law, and so on—because they want to show how exchange and specialization can be structured in the best way. Once again, how can people evaluate assumptions about what is the "best way" to structure an economy? The Christian claim that we were made to steward the world together provides a standard.

This view of economics affirms the goodness of economic relations while standing against the *homo economicus* model. As Christians, we do not need to throw out the basic structures of market economies. Indeed, we must affirm their goodness as part of God's plan, in which people are made to steward the world together in ways that can happen only through economic exchange, ways that are best facilitated by the rule of law and the protection of personal freedoms that are core elements of market economies. But we must oppose, subvert, and overthrow the dominant economic narrative through which these systems are interpreted and structured: the myth of the autonomous, consumption-oriented individual who can be happy without God. This involves reinter-preting the market structures we affirm. We do not simply own and use property, but steward the world by the way we do so; we do not simply exchange with one another, but steward the world together through this process.

THE ECONOMICS OF HOLY WAR

Christianity doesn't just provide standards of right and wrong for economics. It also explains why such standards are so desperately needed—why our economies are so saturated with greed, debt, materialism, dependency, and injustice. When humanity rebelled against God and fell away from him, we didn't stop being stewards of his world. That's the image of God in us, continuing to show how he originally made us even after our spiritual ruin. But al-though fallen people continue to steward the world, they don't have the power and mercy of God in their lives. They can't bring the holy love of God into the world through their stewardship. Instead, they come under the influence of Satan, who can manipulate their feelings of guilt, shame, and fear to accomplish his ends.

This universe is contested territory, claimed as a kingdom by both God and Satan. Their war for kingship focuses on the loy-alty of human beings. Every person who follows God brings their little corner of the world—the part of the world that is under their stewardship—back into the kingdom of God. Every person who rejects God is, in effect, turning over their corner of the world to Satan's kingdom, to be ruled by the power of guilt, shame, and fear rather than by the holy love of the Father, Son, and Spirit. From the household checkbook to the global trade system, our economies are full of afflictions—poverty, injustice, materialism. That is be-cause, since the fall, humanity has been trying to run them on our own power rather than on the power of God's holy love in our lives.

In Christ, as the gospel goes forward with power, God is reclaiming the world from the kingdom of Satan back into the kingdom of God by reclaiming the people who steward the world. That is why, for two thousand years, the Christian faith has been slowly but surely turning the world's economies upside down. As we will see in the chapters ahead, the differences between the economic systems of the first century and the economic systems of the modern world are vast. The positive changes—protection under the law for poor people's rights to work and exchange, abolition of slavery, economic growth—have been in large part the result of the gospel's influence in people's lives.

The negative changes are part of the story too. Satan has found many opportunities to corrupt good economic accomplishments to evil ends. Freedom is used as an opportunity for sin. The great wealth produced by modern economies is used to buy pornography or fund colonial oppression. Wherever Satan sees an opportunity, he does his best to pervert the world's economies. Satan knows that just as sin produces poverty and injustice, poverty and injustice also increase the temptation to further sin. Satan is doing everything he can to prevent real economic flourishing in God's world, just as the power of God in the gospel restores people to righteousness and, by so doing, causes economies to flourish.

The end of the holy war, and thus the final future of our economies, is not in doubt. When Jesus returns, the power of Satan's kingdom will be overthrown. We will once again live as stewards of the world under God and manage the world by the power of God's holy love. We will steward the world together, bringing an end to poverty and injustice so everyone can contribute through their work to the flourishing of God's world.

What is in doubt is how you and I, and our businesses, communities, and nations, will live in the present day. The gospel demands a new economic life. Following Jesus means living in the kingdom of God, managing our little parts of the world as his stewards. Our economic lives—on the job, in household affairs, in the marketplace, and in the public square generally—must put the kingdom of God into action. We cannot do this in a full and complete way until Jesus returns, because we continue to struggle with sin both in our own hearts and in the world around us. But we must bring into the present little sneak previews—foretastes— of the very different kind of economy that King Jesus will fulfill when he returns.

2

JUSTICE AND MERCY

KEY SCRIPTURAL TEACHINGS FOR
ECONOMIC ARRANGEMENTS

Scripture speaks extensively about right and wrong economic arrangements. This demonstrates God's intense concern about these issues, which have such far-reaching effects on our lives. If believers are to be faithful, and if we want to bring the justice and mercy of God to the people around us, we must study what God says and then seek to put it into action as far as our own influence allows. We cannot, however, simply pick up arrangements designed for an ancient agrarian economy and set them down unchanged in our modern postindustrial economy—nor would God want us to do so if we could, for reasons that will become clear below. Our challenge is to "recontextualize" God's teachings for economic arrangements, taking them out of their original context and putting them into practice in the new context of the modern economy.

THE ECONOMIC STORY OF THE OLD TESTAMENT

The Bible begins by telling us that God made human beings to work. We have already seen that God created Adam and Eve to rule the world as good stewards (Gen. 1:27–28). He put them in the garden to work the earth, cultivating its potential and protecting it from being squandered or abused (2:15). But we are also made to rest and enjoy the world God created, appreciating his goodness to us with thankfulness (Ps. 127:2; 1 Tim. 6:17).

One of the most radical teachings in the Bible is that God himself is a worker. We are made to do creative work because God does creative work, and we are made to rest and appreciate God's work because God rests and appreciates his work. Genesis 1–2 depicts God working to make the world. This idea that God is a worker directly contradicts the creation myths of other ancient cultures. In their religions, the universe is chaotic, and our world comes into being as a result of conflicts among primordial forces. There is no divine labor in creation, so there is no creative design giving purpose to our labor. Sometimes our work is even a curse imposed on us— the gods don't want to work, so they create us to work for them.[1]

In the biblical creation account, each day God works to create and then appreciates what he has created. The cycle goes from the creative word "Let there be . . ." to the appreciative word "It is good." Each day this cycle of creation and appreciation is repeated: "Let there be. . . . It is good; Let there be. . . . It is good." This series of six working days culminates in a rest day, on which God surveys all his work and appreciates its supreme excellence: "It is very good."

Our own lives are to be built on this pattern; this is one of the central ways human beings serve as images of God. On each working day we are to work hard for the day, doing good work that bears fruit worthy to be appreciated. In doing so, we join in the ongoing creative work of God as he sustains and cares for his world; in our small and creaturely way, we join our creative work to God's divine creative work. And at the end of the working week we are to enjoy a rest day, on which we can appreciate the goodness and greatness of all the work God has done, both in the original creation and in his ongoing care for us.

We have also seen how we were made to do our work cooperatively. When God saw that it was not good for Adam to do his work

[1] See Timothy Keller and Katherine Leary Alsdorf, *Every Good Endeavor: Connecting Your Work to God's Work* (New York: Dutton, 2012), 34–35.

alone, he created not a mere incubator for children, not a social media site so Adam wouldn't get lonely, but a coworker. Certainly procreation and companionship are part of God's beautiful plan, establishing the intimacy of marriage and the belonging of community. But what Adam needed first and foremost was someone to *work* alongside him, to share the great mission of being good stewards of the world.

Work is not only at the center of God's design for each of us as individuals; it is at the center of how he made us to relate to one another. That is the basis of economic exchange. From a husband and wife splitting up household tasks to the global traders who now bring a quarter billion dollars' worth of wheat from Argentina to Indonesia every year, we all serve each other by trading our work.

Genesis 1–2 provides a social vision of peace and harmony through cooperative work and marriage. Work and marriage—the economy and the family—are the two institutions clearly present in God's design from the beginning. Interestingly, neither politics nor the church is explicitly present at the creation in institutional form. They can be considered as implicitly present, as things that were going to be needed eventually in any case. Or they can be considered as systems that had no distinct existence until after the fall, when conflict and distrust introduced a need for politics, and the unwillingness of some to follow God introduced the first distinction between the church and the world. Either way, the institutions God puts at the center of human life from the beginning are the economy and the family.

After the fall, this vision is ruined. Shame, fear, and distrust destroy the cooperative working relationships we were made to have, bringing injustice and alienation into our working and economic relationships. Work, while it is not itself a curse, is fundamentally transformed because of God's curse on the ground because of sin. Work becomes toilsome, involving both pain and fatigue (Gen. 3:17, 19). Work also becomes futile (v. 18). We encounter the futility of work after the fall on two levels. In the short term, our work can go wrong and fail to be productive. In the long term, even if everything in work goes right, for people cut off from God, the meaning and purpose of their work is not ultimately satisfying (Eccles. 1:1–11).

God, however, intervenes to prevent the ruin of his creatures from becoming a total collapse and to start the process of redeeming a people for himself. From Genesis 4 onward, we see a division between God's people and those who reject him. One of the clearest distinctions is in the economic life of God's people.

Among his people, God works to restore, in a limited way at first, the original social vision of productive work and economic cooperation. The providential and redemptive rule of God over his special people includes careful attention to their economic arrangements. When he brings them into the promised land, he gives them laws, institutions, and arrangements for doing justice and mercy among a people who are deeply inclined toward sin. These provisions are part of the legal codes in Exodus, Leviticus, and Deuteronomy.[2] In addition to prohibitions against theft, fraud, and similar crimes, the proper ownership and use of land is a key concern of these laws. In an agricultural economy, working the land is how people feed themselves and meet one another's needs. This is why it is essential for God's people to understand that their land has been provided to them by God and must be used in the ways God prescribes.[3] Before and after their time in the Holy Land, God sends them guidance on how to work faithfully in the communities—Egypt and Babylon—where they must live in exile (see, for example, Jer. 29:1–7).

Concern for the economically poor is a key theme of Old Testament economic provisions. Care for the poor is identified as a key distinguishing mark of authentic faith. "Whoever oppresses a poor

---

[2] For a detailed review of these laws, see David L. Baker, *Tight Fists or Open Hands? Wealth and Poverty in Old Testament Law* (Grand Rapids, MI: Eerdmans, 2009).

[3] See Christopher J. H. Wright, *Old Testament Ethics for the People of God* (Downers Grove, IL: InterVarsity Press, 2004), 76–99.

man insults his Maker, but he who is generous to the needy honors him" (Prov. 14:31). God gives his people institutions such as the gleaning laws, which require a small amount of the economic production of each field or vineyard be left available for those who have no land of their own on which to gather food through their own work (Lev. 19:9–10; Deut. 24:19–22). We see these laws at work in the story of Ruth and Boaz; the wisdom and goodness of Boaz is especially visible in the care he takes to ensure that economically poor women like Ruth not only have access to gainful work, but are protected from abuse (Ruth 2). The Old Testament's concern for the integrity and authority of kinship structures such as households, clans, and tribes is also relevant here, as these structures have primary responsibility to ensure the poor are cared for. The prophets denounce the monarchy for taking power away from these kinship structures, which have a duty of care to their members, in order to benefit the king.[4]

Notoriously, God's provisions for economic justice among his people do not include a complete removal of the institution of slavery, which is a primary form of economic injustice. Apparently, before the coming of Christ, it is not yet God's time for the abolition of slavery. God's work of refining his people and purifying them of their sin seems long and slow to us, and the continued existence of slavery in any form in the promised land can be baffling. However, it is important to note that while the Old Testament law accommodates the existence of slavery, it does not endorse it. In fact, it limits the practice of slavery in major ways as compared with the laws of surrounding nations.[5]

God's care for his people also includes sending prophets. One function of the prophets is to indict wicked rulers when they disobey God's laws. The economic laws are a special focus of the prophets, attracting the largest share of their prophetic indictments

---

[4] See Keith Reeves, "Family and Opportunity in the Law and the Prophets," Oikonomia Network, May 21, 2018, https://oikonomianetwork.org/resources/family-and-opportunity-in-the-law-and-the-prophets/.
[5] See Baker, *Tight Fists*, 111–95.

and some of their most memorable curses and lamentations. The prophets' emphasis is on the wickedness of kings taking land from the households that rightfully own it. Without land, the households cannot support themselves economically and become dependent on the favor of the powerful for their sustenance.[6] The prophets also share visions that depict a full restoration of God's original social plan of harmony and cooperation, coming after God's chosen one arrives and finishes the work of redemption. The restoration of economic harmony and flourishing is, again, a central prophetic focus (see, for example, Isa. 60).

THE ECONOMIC STORY OF THE NEW TESTAMENT

In the Gospels, Jesus announces that he has come to inaugurate the kingdom of God. He invites people to begin—today, now—living with God as their King.[7] As the incarnation of God, he is the complete revelation of God to humanity, showing us who God is and thus providing a superior standard for understanding how to follow God. He inaugurates the kingdom supremely through his death and resurrection, reconciling sinful people to God, forgiving their sin, and overthrowing the dictatorship that guilt, shame, and fear have set up in their hearts because of sin, so that they have the power to live for God. By doing so, he defeats Satan's power over them and begins the process of reclaiming the world from Satan. "The reason the Son of God appeared was to destroy the works of the devil" (1 John 3:8). He ascends to heaven, pouring out the Holy Spirit in a dramatic new way to increase the power of God's people to live the way they should—fulfilling the promise of the prophets that the chosen one would not just tell God's people to be good, but actually make them good. And he promises to return to complete his work, destroying the kingdom of Satan and extending the kingdom of God over all the earth.

---

[6] See Reeves, "Family and Opportunity."
[7] See Dallas Willard, *The Divine Conspiracy: Rediscovering Our Hidden Life in God* (New York: HarperCollins, 2009).

One of the most immediate and profound effects of choosing to live in God's kingdom is the way it changes our economic life. Our daily work is a primary place where Jesus describes life in the kingdom of God taking place. Of his fifty-two parables, forty-five are set in the world of work—he shows us what the kingdom looks like in fields, vineyards, marketplaces, households, treasuries, palaces, and sheepfolds.[8] He practices what he preaches, living as a worker himself until the time for his public ministry has come; the perfect life that he has to live to be our Savior is apparently a life of carving, stonecutting, thatching, sawing, and hammering. And when the time comes to share his message, he mostly goes into workplaces and marketplaces to share it—122 of the 132 recorded public appearances of Jesus are in the marketplace, and so are thirty-nine of the forty divine interventions recorded in Acts.[9] In addition to doing good work himself, he teaches his people to be honest, frugal, content, and generous in their household management and economic dealings.

Jesus also bears prophetic witness against economic injustice. He arrives in a nation living under oppression from a foreign conqueror, dominated by a small wealthy class of absentee landlords who have fattened themselves by taking all the land away from its rightful owners. Jesus shows love and compassion to the sinners who have practiced this oppression, but he does not compromise with their sin—he confronts it on numerous occasions.[10]

Jesus also confronts the economic exploitation practiced by religious leaders, as in the cleansing of the temple. He regularly comes into conflict with them over Sabbath regulations, which, under their administration, have ceased to function as protections for the day of appreciative rest, and have instead become tools of

---

[8] See R. Paul Stevens, *Work Matters: Lessons from Scripture* (Grand Rapids, MI: Eerdmans, 2012), 134.

[9] See Stevens, *Work Matters*, 134.

[10] See Keith Reeves, "The Testaments Treat Wealth Differently," Oikonomia Network newsletter, April 1, 2015, https://oikonomianetwork.org/2015/04/the-testaments-treat-wealth-differently/.

oppression, preventing people from doing work they need to do. Jesus even reminds us, in the midst of one of these conflicts, that God is a worker and that he, the supreme image of God, is working as well (John 5:17).

When corrupt tax collector Zacchaeus meets Jesus, he responds to Jesus's compassion by paying back everything he has stolen fourfold—the penalty under the law of Moses for especially egregious theft. He then gives away half his remaining wealth to those suffering in poverty under Roman oppression. Jesus announces, "Today salvation has come to this house" (Luke 19:9).

Paradoxically, however, Jesus does not immediately bring about political and economic liberation on a large scale. He certainly could do so—as he says, his Father has legions of angelic warriors ready to descend in an instant if Jesus calls for them (Matt. 26:53). But this is not the way God will reclaim his world, at least for the present age. For now, there will be no visible divine war of liberation. Even when he is asked merely to give his opinion in a legal case over disputed property, Jesus forcefully declines: "Who made me a judge or arbitrator over you?" (Luke 12:14). He does not go anywhere near that kind of role.

Life in the kingdom is a life of faithful apprenticeship to Jesus, including under conditions of economic oppression and depravation. Just as Jesus went to the cross, believers must take up our cross and die daily. That does not mean we are passive in the face of injustice, just as Jesus was not passive in the face of injustice. But neither are we to use brute force and simply suppress or destroy the wicked—for "Vengeance is mine, I will repay, says the Lord" (Rom. 12:19).

This is why the church's instructions for how to live focus on cultivating a faithful life in our work and in the household. The New Testament Epistles, speaking to the church after Jesus's ascension to heaven and the outpouring of the Spirit at Pentecost, often include "household codes" (Eph. 5:22–6:9; Col. 3:18–4:1;

1 Tim. 3:1–13; Titus 2:1–10; 1 Pet. 2:13–3:7). A household code is a typical way to summarize instructions for right living in ancient wisdom literature. The mission of the church, delivered by Jesus himself just before he ascended, is to become disciples (students, apprentices) of Jesus in the way we live, and to help others do the same (Matt. 28:16–20). Doing good work and trading honestly with others is central to the household codes and to the general moral vision of the New Testament.

God's special concern for the poor also continues from the Old Testament into the New without interruption. Jesus identifies the coming of the kingdom of God to the poor as a proof of his credentials as the Messiah, comparable to miraculous healing (Matt. 11:4–5). He says that what you do for the least of his brothers, you do for him (25:40). He admonishes his followers to do good to those who are too poor to repay them, so as to receive a superior repayment from God on the last day (Luke 6:35). So great is Jesus's emphasis on generosity that among his followers, everyone shares with one another to the point where private ownership of property, while it is still present, is radically relativized (Acts 2:42–47).

The New Testament household codes do not abolish slavery, but Paul does urge slaves to seek their freedom (1 Cor. 7:21) and challenges Philemon to set his slave Onesimus free because Christ has set Philemon free (Philem. 8–22). So just as Jesus does not lead an immediate war of liberation, but does stand in opposition to injustices, first-century Christians are not called to rise up immediately and fight a war to abolish slavery, but are urged to free their own slaves (Paul's message to Philemon would obviously apply to every Christian slave owner) and to form a community of people whose witness will stand against slavery. Over time, it is the witness of the church in precisely this way that leads to the abolition of slavery in late antiquity and the early Middle Ages.[11] After slavery

---

[11] See Rodney Stark, *The Victory of Reason: How Christianity Led to Freedom, Capitalism, and Western Success* (New York: Random House, 2005), 26–32.

is reintroduced in the modern world, it is once again the witness of the church in the nineteenth-century abolitionist movement that abolishes it.

This focus on Christian discipleship through faithful work in faithful households does not stand in contrast with the building up of the church as a distinct community. On the contrary, it is deeply in harmony with it. The church is established precisely to build up this kind of life among its members. In his "inaugural address," Jesus points to the preaching of the good news to the poor and the liberation of the oppressed as special signs of the coming of the kingdom (Luke 4:18). In Ephesians 4:11–12, we are told that church leaders are ordained for the purpose of equipping the saints for works of service—that is, for serving faithfully in their tasks in everyday life. Pastors often quote the line in Hebrews 10:25 admonishing us that the church should not neglect to gather together, as is the way of some. What is less noticed is the purpose for which they are to gather, identified in the previous verse. The author of Hebrews says that we gather on Sunday morning not so the pastor and the church staff can provide us with religious goods and services to consume, but "to stir up one another to love and good works" all week (v. 24).

The New Testament also has a heavily eschatological bent, constantly pointing us forward to Jesus's return. The world that Jesus will make when he returns sets the standard for the way we should try to live today, even though we can't fully realize it in our present conditions. We should seek to live as a "sneak preview of coming attractions." And the New Testament vision of that future world emphasizes a restoration of the cooperative work in the Genesis vision (Rev. 21:24–26). The divine war of liberation from economic and political oppression that Jesus does not bring in the present age, not even at the level of giving a legal opinion, is coming in full force when he returns. After that, God's people will be fully restored to good stewardship of the world under God, working together in harmony across all cultural divisions to cultivate and care for God's world (22:5).

RECONTEXTUALIZING: ECONOMICS IN LIGHT OF PENTECOST

Scripture is the supreme authority for Christians. It is how God has chosen to reveal himself redemptively to the church in the present age. So we cannot take Scripture as merely a description of things that have happened in the past. It is that, of course, but is also given to us for the purpose of shaping us in the present. As we confront challenging economic problems in our own time, Scripture is to guide our response—not only because it is perfectly true and trustworthy, although it is; not only because it speaks with God's authority, although it does; but also because by the Holy Spirit, God uses our obedience to Scripture to draw us ever closer into union with himself in Christ. To pay our bills on time, serve our customers well, or support constructive public responses to globalization is, for followers of Jesus, part of the apprenticeship to him that constitutes the mission of the church.

This does not mean, however, that our job is simply to pick up the laws of Moses and put them into practice exactly as they are. We might expect that, just as some of Jesus's earthly contemporaries expected him to lead a revolution and overthrow Rome. But that is not how God works. In fact, his reason for working the way he does is the same in both cases.

God unfolds his plan of salvation in historical stages. Jesus did not overthrow Rome because the time for a divine war of political and economic liberation had not yet come. That will take place when he returns. Similarly, the economic regulations in Exodus and Deuteronomy were part of God's covenant with Moses, governing the life of Israel in the promised land. They were designed for that time and place, with its particular circumstances. They were never intended to govern all people everywhere, because

God's covenant with Moses was not a covenant with all people everywhere.

The biggest change in God's way of dealing with his people at Pentecost. Before the new outpouring of the Holy Spirit that came at Pentecost, God worked with one nation as his special people. If people outside that nation wanted to follow God, they had to travel to Israel and join it—leaving behind their lands and peoples, laws and customs, and even languages. God's people were one nation with one set of laws and one way of life. But in the New Testament, the church is sent out to make disciples of all nations. At Pentecost, people of many nations hear the gospel *in their own languages*. Then they go home to speak and live out the gospel in their own nations, among their own peoples, under their own laws and their own ways of life. Of course they must do so in a faithful way, and that must sometimes put them in opposition to laws and customs in their nations that contradict God. But they will not all be living under one set of laws with one language and one way of life.

The New Testament church is irreducibly diverse, living in many ways. Coping with that diversity was a huge problem for the early church, and many controversies resulted. A large portion of the New Testament is devoted to showing how the apostles responded: by making space for diverse forms of faithfulness (see, for example, Rom. 14:1–15:7). God is redeeming people from every tribe, tongue, and nation so that in the end, every nation on earth will be to him what Israel was in the Old Testament—the people of God (Rev. 21:3).

We continue to live in this post-Pentecost period of the church, and that provides our guiding principle for how to draw on Scripture in the modern world. Our job is not to conquer our nations by force and impose the laws of ancient Israel upon them, any more than it was the job of the Egyptians, Arabs, Romans, and Greeks who were in the room at Pentecost to go back home and conquer

Egypt, Arabia, Rome, and Greece by force and impose the laws of ancient Israel on them. Our job is what their job was: to live faithfully as disciples of Jesus among our nations and to help others do the same. Because there are many nations, there is no one-size-fits-all set of laws or way of life.

All of Scripture shows us what God is like and what God's holy love looks like in action. Even if we don't put the Mosaic laws into practice today, we can still learn lessons about God and his ways by looking at what those laws show us. God is the same God today as he was when he gave those laws to Moses; we might not live under those laws, but we do live under the same God who made them.

One way of thinking about how we can draw lessons for today from Scripture is to look for principles that transfer from the original context to the new one. The Old Testament gleaning laws required the owners of fields or vineyards to leave small portions of their crops unharvested so that poor people who had no land could come harvest food for themselves. The landowners were required to be generous in order to create opportunity, but the poor were not reduced to dependence on handouts—they supported themselves by the work of their own hands. Today, we don't have many farm and vineyard jobs available. But we can call upon those who are economically comfortable to make sacrifices in order to support efforts to give more people an opportunity to work, and where that opportunity is available, we can call on the poor to take it and support themselves. To extend the example, in the book of Ruth we see that landowner Boaz gives orders to ensure that female gleaners will not be sexually harassed in his workplace; in effect, he makes himself the protector who ensures safety and respect for women who do not have local male protectors. This also provides a model for our workplaces. We no longer expect every woman to find herself a male protector, as that ancient culture did, but we should nonetheless institute rules in our workplaces to guard against sexual harassment of women (and men, for that matter).

At a deeper level, in order to know what principles to look for and how to recontextualize them, we need to understand how the original context and the new one differ. That requires understanding redemptive history. We need to see both Scripture and ourselves as part of God's unfolding plan to save the world, which started in the garden with the original promise to Adam and Eve, and will not be completed until Jesus returns. So continuing the example of the gleaning laws, the key difference between the original context and ours is the connection between the land and economic production. Gleaning laws were designed to provide an opportunity for those in poverty to work in an economy where productive labor mostly meant working on a farm, in a vineyard, or in another land-based agricultural enterprise. In the modern economy, economic production is no longer tied to land, which is why we don't glean. We need to find new ways of helping connect people to jobs, such as mentorship programs. Similarly, we don't use a system of male protectors anymore because modern political and economic systems make female independence possible, but we still need to be concerned about sexual harassment (as the headlines make abundantly clear).

This is why the Christian intellectual tradition and its history are so important. It is by looking at this history that we understand such changes as the shift away from land-based economies or the changing role of women in society. Just as important, studying the Christian intellectual tradition helps us understand how these changes relate to the content of Scripture. No individual is smart enough to figure out alone, in isolation, all of the theological implications of (for example) the move away from a land-based economy to an industrial and, finally, a postindustrial economy. We need to learn from all of the church's reflections and actions in history to build up our understanding through earlier Christians' insights.

The story, laws, and promises of the Bible inform our economic life by setting its purpose, meaning, standards, and priorities. The Bible reveals which economic purposes are good and which are not.

The church, under the Bible's teaching, helps people develop a new way of understanding the meaning of things in their lives, and this changes how they understand their daily participation in economic systems. The Bible shows us the protective ethical boundaries that God has laid down as standards for our economic behavior. And the Bible helps us set right priorities, putting first things first.

JUSTICE AND MERCY: INTEGRITY, FRUITFULNESS, PROVISION, COMPASSION

Before we leave this initial biblical survey, it will be useful to sum up some of the Bible's key economic teachings. We will focus on concerns that we find running consistently throughout the Bible, revealing deep patterns in God's care and command for economic affairs.

One of the most consistent and urgent themes of the Bible is that we are to be honest and just in our own dealings, and to find appropriate ways to stand in opposition to dishonest or unjust dealings. The starting point of good economics is to separate ourselves from evil unto good. As Jesus said, a bad tree can't bear good fruit (Luke 6:43).

This remains an essential starting point today. In his masterpiece, *The Divine Conspiracy*, Dallas Willard said our daily work is a primary place where we pursue spiritual formation. When he summed up how Christians should do their jobs, before he got to love for neighbor, prayer, and diligent service, he established integrity as the starting point:

> A gentle but firm noncooperation with things that everyone knows to be wrong, together with a sensitive, nonofficious, nonintrusive, nonobsequious service to others, should be our usual overt manner. This should be combined with inward attitudes of constant prayer for whatever kind of activity our workplace requires and genuine love for everyone involved.[12]

---

[12] Willard, *Divine Conspiracy*, 285–86.

Elsewhere, Willard explained that however important other forms of witness against injustice may be, the most important way to oppose injustice is by not participating in it ourselves—not only because our integrity as followers of Jesus demands it, but because our refusal to participate is, in itself, a powerful force to stop injustice from happening.[13]

A second clear pattern in Scripture is that we should expand opportunities for productive work. People are made in God's image to contribute to God's world through their work (see, for example, Ex. 20:9; 35:30–35; Ps. 90:17; 128:2; Prov. 12:11–14; 16:3; 18:9; 22:29; 24:27; 31:13–31; Eccles. 3:22; 5:6; 9:10; Matt. 25:14–30; Luke 19:11–27; John 5:17; Eph. 4:28; Col. 3:23–24; 1 Thess. 4:11; 2 Thess. 3:10–12; 1 Tim. 5:8; 2 Tim. 2:6). When people are disconnected from work—regardless of whether it is because of their own lack of moral and social formation, unjust social systems, or some combination of factors—our duty is clear. At the personal and social levels, we should be striving to increase opportunities for people to exercise their God-given gifts in work that cultivates and protects God's world.

Tom Nelson points out that "fruitfulness" is a key theme throughout the Bible, from the Genesis 1:22 command to "be fruitful" (which does not refer only to procreation) to Jesus's statement that the world will know we are his disciples because we bear much fruit. Fruitfulness is often interpreted in an exclusively internal way, as if "the fruit of the Spirit" were only a sort of therapeutic self-help tool. But the fruit of the Spirit—love, joy, peace, patience, kindness, goodness, faithfulness, gentleness, and self-control (Gal. 5:22–23)—demands action. Nelson shows that one essential requirement for being fruitful in Scripture's sense is vocational productivity. Whatever arena of service we are in, whether at home, on the job, or anywhere else, vocational pro-

---

[13] See Dallas Willard, *Spirit of the Disciplines: Understanding How God Changes Lives* (San Francisco: Harper & Row, 1988), 220–50.

ductivity means doing good work that makes the world a better place.[14]

A third powerful pattern in Scripture is the importance of supporting our own households economically whenever we are able. This is partly to preserve justice, as the rich can prey upon the poor if they are economically dependent. When poor households support themselves through their own work rather than depending on largesse from the powerful, they have independence and their dignity is respected. This, as we have noted, is the main point of the prophets' indictment of the wicked kings. And it is partly a requirement of neighborly love. When Paul admonishes the Thessalonians not to be idle but to work and support themselves, he doesn't mention the beauty of vocational fruitfulness, contributing to God's world, and preserving a just social order, although he could. Nor does he connect his admonition to eschatology, although he could. Instead, he reminds them sternly that Christian love requires them not to be an unnecessary burden on their productive neighbors:

> Now we command you, brothers, in the name of our Lord Jesus Christ, that you keep away from any brother who is walking in idleness and not in accord with the tradition that you received from us. For you yourselves know how you ought to imitate us, because we were not idle when we were with you, nor did we eat anyone's bread without paying for it, but with toil and labor we worked night and day, that we might not be a burden to any of you. (2 Thess. 3:6–8)

Finally, the duty of compassion for those in need is a clear pattern throughout Scripture. This is a multidimensional duty because there are multiple dimensions of human need. To a large extent, helping those in need overlaps with resisting injustice and expanding opportunities to work for those who are not working. But it goes further. In particular, those who are not able to

---

[14] Tom Nelson, *The Economics of Neighborly Love: Investing in Your Community's Compassion and Capacity* (Downers Grove, IL: InterVarsity Press, 2017).

support themselves through their own work are to be generously cared for. This is primarily a duty of the household, as people in the household who are able to provide support care for those who aren't. Paul states this duty in very strong language: "But if anyone does not provide for his relatives, and especially for members of his household, he has denied the faith and is worse than an unbeliever" (1 Tim. 5:8). But where the household cannot cope with its own needs, the church and the larger community should be called in. This is the implicit principle of the Old Testament concern for kinship structures in Israel and the sharing of property in the early church depicted in Acts 2.

THE CHURCH AND THE WORLD: A CONSTRUCTIVE CONFLICT

As we review these patterns in Scripture to learn what God wants from our economic life, it becomes clear that there is a stark contrast between his standards and what we see going on in the world around us. We are not the first to notice this contrast. In fact, the story of the Christian intellectual tradition is a story of tension between God's standards and the world's standards.

But this has not been a fruitless tension. The encounter between God's word and the world's ways has produced conflict, but not a merely destructive conflict. Through this tension, God's people have built up new and better structures, and ultimately new ways of life that move the world toward what God intends. There have been counterattacks, and our spiritual enemy has often reclaimed ground from the church or found new ways to corrupt and oppress people. Yet the battle never fully goes his way, and we live in the midst of the continuing war. The next several chapters will survey some of the highlights of this story, starting with the first arrival of the gospel among the nations of the world.

3

THE ANCIENT CRISIS

FROM NATURAL TO
SUPERNATURAL ECONOMICS

Before the rise of Christianity, a certain kind of economic and political organization was common to civilizations around the world.
Economic decisions, like decisions in all other areas of life, were
under the control of those at the top. The economy was organized
on the principle that the purpose of every person's work was to
benefit those above them. As Christianity spread, it came into direct
conflict with this system, calling upon those at the top to work to
serve others, including those below them, rather than exploiting the
powerless. Christians organized new economic institutions, such
as hospitals, designed to meet the needs of those at the bottom. In
some other respects, however, Christian thought was influenced by
the economic ideas and practices of the surrounding cultures; these
areas of cultural conformity would be challenged later on.

"NATURAL" SOCIAL ORDER

Today, it is becoming more difficult to describe the ways in which
the cultures of the world are similar. Increased emphasis on cultural differences—often very justified—has left many with a suspi-
cion that any attempt to observe similarities is really just foisting
the view of one culture on all the others. Certainly the history of
colonialism justifies a degree of caution about overgeneralizing,
and it's healthy for all of us to be mindful that each of us, as an

individual, can assimilate only so much information about other cultures. Nonetheless, in the field of economics, we continue to see strong evidence that some things really are universal.

Some broad generalizations about the ways civilizations organize their economies have survived skepticism, because the evidence supports them. To some extent this is because human beings are natural creatures as well as cultural creatures. Cultures vary, but nature is the same, because it's God's design. Some ways of using resources really are more efficient than others, always and everywhere, because nature is just built that way. That is why, for example, all societies in known history have practiced some kind of economic specialization, and societies tend to become more economically specialized as they grow.

There is another and more troubling way in which nature produces universal economic phenomena. When we talk about "nature," we sometimes mean nature as God made it—good. But sometimes, and especially when we talk about human nature, we don't mean nature as God made it but nature as it is now, after the fall, infected with sin and corrupted by the power of evil. Fallen human nature has ubiquitous qualities—greed, sloth, pride, envy, gluttony, lust, and wrath—that shape the ways economies work. This kind of nature is the same always and everywhere not because of God's design but because sinners can't overcome their own sin; the fallen world can't redeem itself.

This double sense of the term *nature* as the way God made things and the shape they've gotten into since the fall helps us understand why a certain kind of political and economic system was common to all ancient societies. In a seminal analysis, Douglass North and his coauthors actually call this kind of system "the natural state," because it is the way all societies were organized until, relatively late in history, another kind of order was invented.[1]

---

[1] Douglass C. North, John Joseph Wallis, and Barry R. Weingast, *Violence and Social Orders: A Conceptual Framework for Interpreting Recorded Human History* (New York: Cambridge University Press, 2009), 30.

North uses the term *natural* without a theological meaning, but when we look at his analysis, we should bear in mind the double-edged nature of *nature* that we are aware of as Christians.

North and his coauthors also refer to "the natural state" as "the limited access order." This term emphasizes its most important feature: social structures were organized to limit access to power and leadership as strictly as possible. An elite class of decision makers, roughly 2 percent of the population, maintained monopoly control of social order. Political decisions were made by a small group of political elites; religious decisions by a small group of religious elites; economic decisions by economic elites; and so forth.[2]

The system was able to protect its dominance because elites in each area protected one another's turf. If anyone outside the political elite tried to access political leadership—such as by starting a popular movement in opposition to the chief or king—that person would be opposed not only by the political elites but by religious, economic, intellectual, artistic, and other elites as well. Those at the top of society formed a common front to keep everyone else under their control.

For those of us who have lived all our lives in modern cultures, it is difficult to recapture what the natural, limited-access state of human culture was like. Those at the bottom, who did the work, could not make most decisions about their own lives, even at the most personal level. They belonged to their superiors and had to do the work assigned to them and live under their superiors' management. They had little to no independence or protection for their rights in any area of life. Only a tiny group of people at the top could control their own activities and enjoy protection for their personal rights in the way that we now take for granted as normal.

Some may want to object that nothing has really changed, that those who have power strive to keep it and to keep others out just as

---

[2] See North, Wallis, and Weingast, *Violence*, 30–75.

much today as in the ancient world. That is generally true, but the fact that the powerful act unjustly is not the main point here. Elites keeping a monopoly on power is not viewed as normal and right in the modern world. Even as elites scheme to protect their power, they hide this fact and claim to support the rights of all people, because that is what is viewed as right in modern culture. Our institutions are not built on the assumption that the ironfisted rule of elites over all others is the way things are supposed to be, and that everyone agrees it is the way things are supposed to be—quite the contrary. However short we may fall of our ideals in practice, our social order is built on public norms that affirm equal rights for all people and aspire—at least in principle—to protect those rights under an impartial rule of law.

"NATURAL" ECONOMICS

The economies of ancient societies were organized around the limited-access principle. As a result, the ancient economies were very different from the economies we know today.

Ancient economies were agrarian, dominated by farming. Economic productivity was effectively limited by access to land. If you didn't have access to land, you couldn't produce. If you did, the amount you could produce was more or less determined by how much and what kind of land you had access to. This meant economic power was concentrated in the hands of big landowners.

Almost all economic production took place within households. The household was not limited to a single family but could contain dozens or even hundreds of people, ranging from slaves to tenant farmers to skilled craftsmen to managers. The head of the household—the landowner—had essentially unlimited power over the organization and management of its affairs.

The economies remained agrarian partly because of limited technology, but a more important factor was the limited-access order. There was no opportunity to develop other modes of economic production because that would threaten the power of the big landowners. Any attempt to develop an alternative form of economic production would have met opposition not only from the big landowners but from their allies among the political, religious, and intellectual elites. As we will see in chapter 5, it was when the power structures of the limited-access order finally began to crack that other modes of economic production emerged.

Another feature of the limited-access order was the very limited scope of economic exchange. Ancient societies were largely closed to outsiders and were strictly tradition-bound. This was partly because such isolation was necessary for the elites to exclude rival sources of power. As a result, people mostly engaged in economic exchange only with a very limited set of others—those whom they knew personally or who were at least part of their cultural group. There was some international trade, but it was a very small portion of the total economy. Almost all buying and selling took place within small groups.

Economic roles were assigned to people based on birth, and there was rarely an opportunity to change. If your father was a slave in the fields, you would probably live your whole life as a slave in those same fields. If your father was a village carpenter, you would probably live your whole life as a carpenter in that village. If your father was the owner of a large estate, you would probably live your whole life as the heir, and then the owner, of that estate. And if you moved around in the economic system at all, you would almost certainly not move upward. You might move downward if you made the wrong choices. If you were lucky, you might succeed in moving sideways—into a different role at about the same social rank. The limited-access order made moving upward virtually impossible. (The Bible stories of dramatic social ascent—Joseph, Moses, Daniel—were breathtaking to their original audiences. We read a story about a criminal becoming a court advisor or a Jewish baby being adopted into the royal house, and it hardly fazes us; in the ancient world, these things were like water running uphill.)

There were, of course, exceptions to this general rule. And the higher up you started in the system, the more likely you were to find opportunities to move around, and even to climb. The great theologian Augustine, before his conversion to Christianity, worked his way up as a teacher and scholar from relative obscurity in one of Rome's far-flung provinces to a successful career among the elite in Italy. But that was possible for him because he was born into the educated, comfortable class and his father was able to invest in his education at schools that provided a fast track into the Roman elite. And even then, Augustine's ambitions required enormous effort and sacrifice.[3] The rule was hierarchy and knowing your place; social mobility was the rare and costly exception.

Finally, as a result of the factors noted above, this economic system did not produce economic growth or even enough wealth to ensure survival. Most of the population lived at subsistence level— barely enough to live on—and many people were vulnerable to starvation if there was a drought, a natural disaster, a war, or just a bad harvest. A typical scholarly analysis found that 68 percent of the population in the first-century Roman Empire lived at or below the level of secure subsistence, and another 22 percent were close enough to that level to be in danger in a bad year.[4] This was typical of economies under the limited-access order.[5]

WHY IS THIS "NATURAL"?

Why is this economic system "natural" in cultures around the world? It is partly for reasons having to do with nature in the origi-

---

[3] See Peter Brown, *Augustine of Hippo: A Biography* (Berkeley, CA: University of California Press, 2000), 7–61.

[4] Peter Oaks, "Using Economic Evidence in Interpretation of Early Christian Texts," in *Engaging Economics: New Testament Scenarios and Early Christian Reception*, ed. Bruce W. Longenecker and Kelly D. Liebengood (Grand Rapids, MI: Eerdmans, 2009), 30.

[5] See Joyce Appleby, *The Relentless Revolution: A History of Capitalism* (New York: Norton, 2011), 5–6; and Angus Maddison, *Contours of the World Economy, 1–2030 AD: Essays in Macro-Economic History* (New York: Oxford University Press, 2007), Table A.7, 382.

nal sense. However, the fallenness of human nature is an unavoidable factor.

North and his coauthors emphasize that the limited-access order was our natural state because stability was the overriding concern. In an agricultural economy where the amount of wealth doesn't grow over time, the survival of society itself is constantly in danger. Without a strong central authority to deal with emergencies and ensure that everyone cooperates during times of adversity, panic and chaos would set in. Someone has to make sure the able-bodied men show up for combat duty when bandits and enemies attack, and see to it people don't hoard food during a drought while their neighbors starve. The authoritarian system that suppresses growth, and thus keeps some people on the brink of starvation, also ensures that everyone else gets to live.[6]

That is fair enough as far as it goes, but it raises some deeper questions. Why is it the natural state of humanity to be so distrustful of each other that we have to organize society on the expectation that everyone will shirk or hoard during a crisis? Why is fear of death such an overwhelming force in human life that until recently, people around the world, regardless of cultural differences, have turned to drastic solutions—have sold their freedom and submitted to degrading tyrannies if only they might gain a marginal increase in their chance of survival? Why is it that until recently, every culture on earth was mostly closed to economic trade with outsiders because of xenophobia?

Dualistic systems of religion and philosophy also played a role. In order to protect themselves from the holiness of God, human cultures not influenced by a Christian presence tend to develop a strict conceptual separation between spirit and matter. The mind or soul—the spiritual part of us—is one kind of thing, and lives in its own sphere of activity. The body is separate, and operates in a completely different sphere of activity. Connections between the

---

[6] North, Wallis, and Weingast, *Violence*, 51–54.

two are tenuous. Human culture tends to gravitate toward this kind of thinking because it allows us to keep God safely walled off on the "spirit" side, where he doesn't interfere with what we do with our bodies (i.e., how we actually live and all the things we actually do). This way of thinking very naturally lends itself to a division of labor between people who live the life of the mind (rulers, priests, landowners, philosophers, artists) and people who must work with their bodies.

This division is hierarchical and very demeaning to human dignity. Just as the mind controls the body, the leisure class must control the working class. Aristotle wrote that no one who works for a living ought to be allowed to vote, because such people do not have the time to engage in the activities (politics, religion, philosophy, art) that elevate a person's mind and moral virtue. Anyone who works for a living is not fully human for Aristotle; such people are "tools" (his word) in the hands of their masters, who use them to accomplish the tasks that they, the virtuous thinkers, have discerned are right.[7]

The whole ethos of life in this kind of social order—the way people are taught to think about themselves—is that you exist solely to serve those above you. Your purpose in life is to serve your superiors and do work that contributes to the goals they view as worthwhile and valuable. That principle structured everything in society from the top downward, and all of a person's daily tasks were determined by their place in the hierarchy and the desires of those immediately above them.

SUPERNATURAL ECONOMICS

Jesus began his public ministry by going to the synagogue and reading a passage from Isaiah in which the Messiah says that God "has anointed me to proclaim good news to the poor. He has sent me to proclaim liberty to the captives and recovering of sight to the blind,

[7] Aristotle, *Politics* (New York: Penguin, 1992), 63–65 (I.iv) and 183–185 (III.v).

to set at liberty those who are oppressed, to proclaim the year of the Lord's favor" (Luke 4:18–19). When John the Baptist asked Jesus if he was the Messiah, he said one of the signs proving it was that "the poor have good news preached to them" (Matt. 11:5). The coming of the Savior did not just save souls; it introduced a new way of life into the world, one that brought not only spiritual hope and deliverance but also temporal hope and deliverance to those most in need of it. While "the poor" in the New Testament includes more than just the economically poor, they are one of the primary groups in view.[8]

When the church arrived in the Mediterranean world, it challenged the existing economic order at a fundamental level. It did so because that order was built for sinful people and operated on sinful principles. It was not that there was anything especially sinful about people in the Mediterranean—if the church had arrived first in China, central Africa, or the Americas, it would have found substantially the same economic system there. The whole world was hopelessly mired in sin, and thus in political and economic oppression, until the Holy Spirit brought the good news that made another way possible.

The challenge of the church was not merely to this or that particular economic practice, but to the underlying ethos or mind-set of the whole system. Everything in the system was designed on the principle that people existed to serve those above them, and that was exactly the principle the Christians demanded be reversed. The people at the bottom did not exist to serve the people at the top. Everyone exists to glorify God and show holy love for God and neighbor, so in terms of economic work, everyone is supposed to be working to serve everyone else. But insofar as anyone should be singled out as having a special duty to serve others most self-sacrificially, it is not the poor but the rich! Having more power,

---

[8] See Keith Reeves, "The Testaments Treat Wealth Differently," Oikonomia Network newsletter, April 1, 2015, https://oikonomianetwork.org/2015/04/the-testaments-treat-wealth-differently/.

they have more opportunity to do good for others, and also more temptation to serve themselves.[9]

Paradoxically, because the challenge of the church was at such a deep level, the church was able to adapt itself to daily economic life fairly well. Christians didn't have to separate themselves from the economies of the cultures in which they lived. Some important Christian voices did advocate such separation, but that view did not become the norm.[10] For the most part, Christians worked in those economies alongside their pagan neighbors in every role from field workers and craftsmen to intellectuals and stewards of great houses.[11] The church called on its members to go about their economic work with a fundamentally different understanding of what it was, what it was for, and how it was to be done. Christians were not to be conformed to the ways of the world, which were doomed to die out when Christ came back. They were to live as present-day signposts of the future social order of holiness, peace, and love that would reign supreme upon Christ's return.

Of course, Christians did not always follow this call to live out their faith as they participated in the economy (i.e., they were conformed to the world in the way they participated in the economy). Therefore, participation in the economy in the pagan world was seen, rightly, as a potential source of idolatry and loss of Christian identity.

However, to the extent that Christians did do their economic work in a Christian way, their extensive integration in the economy made them a dangerous threat to the existing order. They were not off in some corner doing their own thing, like so many other religious sects in that very pluralistic social world. They were right there in mainstream society, doing the same jobs as everyone else— but demonstrating that those jobs could be done in a very different

---

[9] See Helen Rhee, *Loving the Poor, Saving the Rich: Wealth, Poverty, and Early Christian Formation* (Grand Rapids, MI: Baker Academic, 2012), 1–48.
[10] See Rhee, *Loving*, 159–89.
[11] See Rhee, *Loving*, 40–48, 159–67.

way, a way that glorified God and served God and neighbor, rather than glorifying and serving social elites.

Christian identity demanded economic life characterized by excellent performance, generous giving, hospitality to strangers, reciprocal recognition, and mutual contribution. Whereas wealthy pagans gave gifts to the poor as a way of establishing superiority and control over them, Christians were to give without expectation of return and were to view all people as fellow workers.[12] Christians did such an excellent job in their work that even during periods when Christianity was under legal persecution, a striking number of Christians remained in prominent positions of economic, social, and even political responsibility.[13] At a time when the standard practice during a plague was to leave the sick to die in isolation, Christians stood out for their willingness to risk their own lives to care for those who were ill. These medical missions created the first hospitals, and Christians gained great standing for the gospel in their societies by caring not only for their own sick people, but for all sick people.[14]

EARLY CHRISTIANITY'S BLIND SPOTS

Christian thinking develops over time; that is what the Christian intellectual tradition is. So it is not surprising that the church did not instantly figure out all the ways in which the world's economic systems were deficient. In some ways, we even see worldly patterns of thinking in early Christian views of economics that had to be rooted out later.

Two further things can be said in defense of the early Christians on this point. One is a reminder that the kind of economic system we have been describing was the norm in every culture that had ever been known. No one had yet imagined a full-scale alternative, so

[12] See Rhee, *Loving*, 103–38.
[13] See Rhee, *Loving*, 43–46.
[14] See Gary Ferngren, "A New Era in Roman Health Care," *Christian History* 101 (2011): 6–12; Timothy S. Miller, "Basil's House of Healing," *Christian History* 101 (2011): 13–16.

naturally many of the specific features of this system seemed inevitable and unchangeable, even to those who knew that the overall ethos was radically wrong. The other is that it took several centuries for Christians to move up enough in the Roman world to have any kind of serious power to push large-scale economic reforms. We cannot fault them if they focused their attention on questions that they had some power to do something about and left the business of figuring out what large-scale economic reform would look like to future generations of Christians who would actually have the power to seek such reforms.

One limitation in early Christian approaches to the dominant economic system was in the way the church evaluated the system's lack of social mobility and its practice of assigning people to social roles based on birth. Some voices, as we have noted, were so offended by the injustice of the world's economic systems that they said Christians must withdraw from the economy completely. They spoke as if wealth were intrinsically evil, or as if it were absolutely impossible to be godly and have wealth at the same time. Among those who accepted economic participation, the focus was on godly behavior of individual Christians within the system rather than reform of the system itself to extend greater economic opportunity. Ultimately, both these approaches were inadequate. Christianity would later develop approaches that emphasized legitimate participation in the world's economic systems, coupled with an ongoing concern to reform them at the systemic level while maintaining personal piety. Of course, people who advocate complete withdrawal and people who practice pietistic participation without systemic concern are still very much with us. But the Christian intellectual tradition from the Middle Ages forward now weighs against them.

Another limitation was that there had never been any other kind of economy in the world besides an agricultural economy. All economic production is closely tied to land in such an economy, so those who have never known any other system tend to develop economic thinking that simply identifies economic opportunity with ownership or control over land. Simple as this may seem, it has far-reaching consequences. It creates an expectation that economies cannot grow very much over time, since the amount and type of land available is permanently fixed. Any real estate agent will tell you, "Buy land, it's the only thing they're not making more of." The assumption that economies could not grow shaped the entire architecture of economic thinking before the late Middle Ages. This is what lay behind many economic ideas, such as the moral prohibition against charging interest on money loans, that would later need to be revised or abandoned when the traditional agricultural economy gave way to new and more dynamic economic arrangements.

A key theme in the next several chapters of this book will be the story of the church awakening to these limitations. As Christianity grew and spread, the tension between the danger of futile withdrawal and the danger of complacent captivity forced the church to develop more constructive approaches. And these new approaches played a critical role in the eclipse of the old agricultural economy and the emergence of something completely different.

4

THE MEDIEVAL CRISIS

FROM CONVENTIONAL TO REFORMING ECONOMICS

During the millennium when Christianity was dominant in Europe, Christians gradually moved beyond simply championing the poor and challenging obvious injustices. They began to rethink the deep structures of the economy, calling into question more and more of the assumptions on which the natural limited-access order was built. The scholastic movement reconsidered traditional church positions on the moral issues involved in trade, growth, and lending. This reconsideration slowly opened up space for new approaches to economics. Social conventions ceased to be simply taken as given; ongoing reform of social practices became normal by the end of the Middle Ages. In the late medieval and early modern era, the pace of social reform increased. Changes to the traditional economy were also championed by new philosophies that emerged from the humanist movement.

HOW MANY ECONOMISTS CAN DANCE ON THE HEAD OF A PIN?

One of the most well-known developments of the Middle Ages is scholasticism, a new kind of philosophy and theology that sought to build up a systematic body of knowledge over time. The scholastics' ambition was to figure out what could be known—about pretty much everything one could know about. They considered every question, from theology and metaphysics to astronomy and law. Of course, no one person or even one generation could accomplish this. Scholasticism had a vision of building up knowledge over time, from generation to generation.

Across Europe, special schools were founded to house this audacious undertaking. For the most part, the universities developed from these schools. The term *university* comes from the scholastics' desire to understand everything that could be known— to build a body of knowledge that would be a single, systematic whole.

It was in their investigations of moral philosophy that the scholastics developed extensive theories about how the economy ought to work. Moral philosophy was a key subject for them. It presented all kinds of interesting intellectual challenges. And of all the fields they studied, moral philosophy had perhaps the most immediate practical value. Wrongs could be righted and justice could be advanced if the church gained a clearer understanding of ethics and morals.

The scholastics were highly disciplined and followed rigid methods of thought. This was necessary to the multigenerational nature of their project. If a fourteenth-century scholastic was going to consider something said by an eleventh-century scholastic—and not just evaluate it, but build upon it in a single intellectual system—then the scholastics had to keep using the same terminology and analyze questions with the same methods across the centuries.

As a result, the scholastics sometimes produced extremely elaborate and complex theories that seemed detached from the real world and its practical concerns. And it became easy to mock the scholastics as useless armchair theorists. The great scholastic Thomas Aquinas considered whether it is possible for more than one angel to be in the same place at the same time; a century later, a book of mystical devotion titled *Sister Catherine* was making fun of such speculative inquiries: "Doctors declare that in heaven, a thousand angels can stand on the point of a needle."[1] This is probably where we get our familiar jibe about "debating how many angels can dance on the head of a pin."

There was a lot of truth in the charge that the scholastics could be out of touch. But they also produced invaluable advances in many fields of inquiry. While there had been philosophers and theologians for centuries, no one had ever undertaken to think in such a systematic and disciplined way—and to do so over centuries, carefully building up knowledge. Today we take it for granted that human knowledge in each subject grows over time, because communities of inquiry maintain bodies of knowledge about those subjects and are always seeking out the next question to ask. It was the scholastics who invented these communities of inquiry.

Economics was one of the fields in which their contributions were essential. Economics as a discipline emerged from the study of moral philosophy in the scholastic tradition. The founding father of modern economics, Adam Smith, was a moral philosopher. And unlike ethicists today, the scholastics didn't have a body of knowledge built up for them by an academic field called *economics*. They effectively *invented* the field of economics, developing many of the key concepts economists still use as part of their investigation of moral philosophy.

JUST PRICES AND TRADE

As we have seen, exchange is central to economics. Forms of exchange, such as buying and selling, are one of the primary ways people manage their resources to get the most out of them. By doing a lot of exchanging with others, we can greatly magnify our power to accomplish our goals.

One of the most important contributions of the scholastics, growing out of their Christian theology, was to put the question

[1] See E. D. Sylla, "Swester Katrei and Gregory of Rimini: Angels, God, and Mathematics in the Fourteenth Century," in *Mathematics and the Divine: A Historical Study*, ed. T. Koetsier and L. Bergmans (Amsterdam: Elsevier, 2005), 251.

of justice at the forefront of our thinking about exchange. Earlier moral thinkers, such as Plato and Aristotle, had not spent much time on the question of what is a just or unjust exchange. They were very interested in the general question "What is justice?" but less in the specific question "What is just in economic exchange?" Obviously they understood that things such as theft were wrong. And a few particular issues, such as what kinds of lending were permissible, did attract attention from some thinkers. On the whole, however, moral philosophers had left traditional markets to function pretty much as they were in the limited-access order.

By contrast, the Christian God's stern demand for justice and love in all things compelled the scholastics to begin examining economic exchange in more detail. They examined questions about price, the information available to the parties of exchanges, and many other factors. Their goal was to describe clearly and precisely what conditions had to be met for an exchange to be just.

Like the early church, the scholastics were typically wary of the dangers of wealth. This made them skeptical about commerce as a way of life. Aquinas wrote that buying and selling as a full-time job "feeds the acquisitive urge which knows no limit but tends to increase to infinity."[2]

But Aquinas also recognized that everyone (except, he thought, the clergy) needs to engage in some commerce in order to tend to the business of life. The farmer or craftsman needs to make "moderate business profits" to provide for the needs of his own household, to "help the poor," and even for civic purposes, such as to "ensure that the country does not run short of essential supplies." So making a monetary profit from buying and selling is fine, as long as you make money to use it for good purposes and "not for its own sake."[3]

[2] Thomas Aquinas, *Summa Theologica* (New York: Blackfriars and McGraw-Hill, 1975), 229–31 (Second Part of the Second Part, Question 77, Article 4). I am deeply indebted to Michael Wittmer for his careful analysis of Aquinas's treatment of just prices and exchange; see Michael Wittmer, "Is a Just Price Enough?" *Journal of Markets and Morality* 20, no. 2 (Fall 2017): 263–78.

[3] Aquinas, *Summa Theologica*, 229–31 (Second Part of the Second Part, Question 77, Article 4).

Today, it is widely believed that the scholastics thought there was an objective "just price" for any given good or service. This is a myth. None of the major scholastics held this view. In fact, some scholastics attacked the idea of an objective just price because it was used to exploit customers. Craftsmen's guilds used their monopoly on the production of manufactured goods to fix prices, fleecing customers unfairly, and justified it with claims that they had to rig the prices in order to ensure a just price.[4]

In fact, one of the key contributions of scholasticism to the development of economics was its formulation of an account of justice in pricing that did not require the calculation of an objective just price. The value of any given economic resource can differ enormously depending on who is using it, how they are using it, and why they are using it. To a connoisseur of fine wine, who has trained his palate to appreciate the qualities of the best vintages, one bottle might be much more valuable than another. To a beginner, all wine tastes pretty much the same, so any given bottle is worth more or less the same as any other. There is no objectively calculable just price for a bottle of fine wine, because its value depends on who drinks it—and the same goes for any other economic good or service.

Justice in exchange, Aquinas explained, is a matter of the conditions under which the exchange occurs rather than the price. Any given good or service might be justly sold either at a surprisingly high price or at a surprisingly low price, if the right conditions are present.

The overarching rule, Aquinas said, is the Golden Rule: Do unto others as you would have them do unto you. "Nobody wants anything to be sold to him for more than it is worth. Therefore nobody should sell something to another for more than it is worth."[5] Since there is no single objective "worth" for all buyers and sellers, each party needs to be able to evaluate the worth of the thing being sold based on accurate information. Therefore, it is wrong to misinform the other party,

---

[4] See Raymond de Roover, "The Concept of the Just Price," *Journal of Economic History* 18, no. 4 (December 1958): 418–34.
[5] Aquinas, *Summa Theologica*, 215 (Second Part of the Second Part, Question 77, Article 1).

or even to knowingly take advantage of the other party's erroneous beliefs. As examples of unjust exchange, he cites buying a metal object for a low price because the seller mistakenly thinks it's brass when you know that it's really gold, or buying a manuscript for a low price because the seller isn't aware that it's rare and valuable.[6]

On the other hand, the buyer and seller need not fully download to each other all possible information that might be relevant. That would be an impossible standard. Thus, Aquinas says, for example, that "strict justice" does not require a wheat seller to disclose that a big shipment of wheat is about to arrive in town, which would depress the price of wheat.[7] Aquinas may have in mind a distinction between information about the nature of the thing itself (which must be disclosed or corrected) and information about the larger context in which the exchange is happening (which need not be disclosed). He particularly seems to treat information about the future as different from information about the present—perhaps because the future is inherently uncertain.

Aquinas's rules do not always make the boundaries of justice totally clear. And the Christian intellectual tradition has debated just how far buyers and sellers are obligated to go in disclosing information. It has also debated how far society ought to go in attempting to enforce the Golden Rule by law. Nonetheless, Aquinas's basic outline—justice in exchange doesn't mean calculating a single objective just price, but buying and selling in a way that allows both parties to achieve their legitimate goals—has been formative for Christian thinking about economic markets.

THE RIGHTS REVOLUTION AND ECONOMIC DEVELOPMENT

Scholastic economics began to work a change in the way people thought about economic systems and economic life. This began

---

[6] Aquinas, *Summa Theologica*, 221 (Second Part of the Second Part, Question 77, Article 2).
[7] Aquinas, *Summa Theologica*, 223–25 (Second Part of the Second Part, Question 77, Article 3).

with challenges to unjust hierarchies of power. However, ongoing concern about abuse of power led slowly toward broader and deeper changes. These changes culminated in the first emergence of sustained economic growth, a development that was to remake the face of the world.

The challenges to injustice in medieval Christian thought grew organically out of the concerns of the early church. As we saw in the previous chapter, when Christianity first encountered the limited-access order, it challenged some of that order's most obvious injustices, especially its general principle that those at the top should rule everything for their own sake, without concern for those at the bottom. In the Middle Ages, concern to restrain the use of power by those at the top became more regular and systematic. First in Italy and later in parts of northern Europe, households with lots of wealth began to feel safe investing their money in new enterprises without having to worry that whatever they built would simply be stolen by princes and rulers. The first economic firms, such as banks and investment companies, began to emerge. One sociologist describes the founding of "the first Italian supercompany" in the 1230s.[8]

As this work of restraining the powerful developed, the idea of "natural rights" emerged in Christian thought. Since at least Augustine in the early fifth century, Christians had spoken of a moral "law of nature" by which all people know what is right and wrong, at least when it comes to how they should treat each other, regardless of whether they have ever received a special revelation from God, such as the Bible.[9] Over the course of the Middle Ages, Christian thinkers worked out the implications of this natural law. They used the phrase "natural right" to describe the right conduct required by the natural law. In the twelfth century, this language began to take on personal significance. Scholastic teachers began to speak about "natural right" as something that individuals could

---

[8] Rodney Stark, *The Victory of Reason: How Christianity Led to Freedom, Capitalism, and Western Success* (New York: Random House, 2005), 117–20.
[9] Augustine, *City of God* (New York: Penguin, 1984), 868 (XIX.12).

claim—a zone of personal freedom for each individual that the natural law requires us to respect.[10] The idea of natural law was that there were certain things that were always wrong to do, such as murder and theft. The idea that people have natural rights is an extension of that idea, because there is something about human beings—something intrinsic to human nature—that makes it always wrong to treat them in wrongful ways. Hence, rights correspond to duties; if you have a duty not to murder me, I have a right not to be murdered by you.[11]

The idea of rights would become revolutionary later, in the modern world. During the Middle Ages, though, its most important effect was to change the way the wealthy treated each other. This change, which at first seemed small, gradually built up systemic economic reforms with major implications.

Rights became the foundation of growing international commerce and the establishment of the first banks and other economic firms in the late Middle Ages. Under the limited-access order in its conventional form, political elites (the nobility) could simply take what they wanted from non-elites. This prevented sustained accumulation of wealth by anyone other than the political elites and limited the viability of international commerce. But by the thirteenth century, prominent households in cities such as Venice and Genoa found that they could build up wealth and reliably keep it because their property rights would be protected. They began to invest in increasing trade with other cities around the Mediterranean and, via Middle Eastern trade routes, the whole known world. They also founded banks and other independent economic entities (firms) to manage their growing commerce.[12]

---

[10] See Brian Tierney, *The Idea of Natural Rights: Studies on Natural Rights, Natural Law, and Church Law 1150–1625*, Emory University Studies in Law and Religion (Grand Rapids, MI: Eerdmans, 1997), 43–77.

[11] For an outstanding contemporary defense of rights theory from a Christian standpoint, see Nicholas Wolterstorff, *Journey toward Justice: Personal Encounters in the Global South* (Grand Rapids, MI: Baker, 2013), 37–118.

[12] See Stark, *Victory*, 69–99.

With these developments, space even began to open up for lending money at interest. This was an even bigger development because it greatly increased the ability of the emerging investor class to launch new economic ventures. At first, this practice grew at the margins of society and in the shadows—Jews were permitted to lend at interest in some places, and some Christians lent money at interest surreptitiously. The results were surprising. Traditional Christian teaching held that lending money at interest was something the rich did to oppress the poor, to take advantage of the poor's lack of access to money. But now, relatively *wealthy* people were taking out loans in order to build up business ventures. The results of making money available to people who could use it productively, and who could afford to take a loss if a new venture didn't work out, were not destructive. They were productive. Slowly and with great hesitation, but with increasing confidence over time, scholastics began to reconsider the absolute prohibition on lending money at interest. They drew new distinctions between exploitative "usury" that destroyed the poor and productive lending that empowered people to take advantage of new opportunities while taking responsible risks.[13]

There was a dark side to the rights revolution, one that is tied up with the history of slavery and colonialism. It is not simply that, at first, rights were not extended to all people. Worse than that, as wealth and power grew, the divide between those who were recognized as having rights and those who were not yet recognized as having them grew more stark and brutal. Even as Europe extended increasing recognition of the rights of its wealthy households, and then of its middle-class households, it used the new wealth and power generated by that recognition of rights to sail around the world exploiting and enslaving non-European peoples. The recognition of those peoples' rights would not come until much later.

---

[13] See Stephen Grabill, "Editor's Introduction," in *Sourcebook in Late-Scholastic Monetary Theory*, ed. Stephen Grabill (Lanham, MD: Lexington Books, 2007), xiii–xxxv.

By the time it came, the economic and political structures built by the rights revolution had become complicit in centuries of colonial injustice. This is what lies behind our polarized historical memory of economic development. Some now look back on the institutions developed by the rights revolution—culminating in what we now call "capitalism," which has its roots in medieval economic development—as tremendous engines of liberation for the oppressed. Others see them as uniquely dangerous sources of oppression. In a sense, both are right.

THE TWO FACES OF HUMANISM— BROTHER MARTIN AND MACHIAVELLI

As we have noted, the scholastic method did have limitations and weaknesses. The scholastics had a tendency to lose touch with real life in complex abstraction. They neglected, and even looked down upon, areas of study where knowledge could not be highly systematized, whether that meant history and literature or (at the time) medicine and engineering. And because their goal was to build up knowledge over time, for the most part they stopped reading older texts altogether. Classical philosophers and historians, the church's early theologians, and the original Hebrew and Greek texts of Scripture went almost completely unread. Even the Latin Bible was not as widely read as one might think, outside the world of specialized scholars, for the simple reason that before printing presses, there were not many copies to go around.

By the late Middle Ages, people were becoming more and more dissatisfied with scholasticism. A new movement that would come to be known as "humanism" championed a different approach. It held up disciplines scholasticism had neglected, arguing that the study of unsystematic fields such as history and literature, and practical arts such as medicine and engineering, would *humanize* the abstract technicalities of scholastic knowledge. (This is why, to this day, such disciplines as history and literature are known as "the humanities.")

And in the fields scholasticism had specialized in—metaphysics, theology, moral philosophy, astronomy, and law—humanism advocated radically different methods. Especially, the humanists went back and read the old books (including classical Greco-Roman philosophy and history, the Bible, and the early church fathers) to see what insights might have been lost in the scholastic synthesis. Their Latin motto was *ad fontes*: "Back to the sources!"

The humanist movement contributed two major new forces that would reshape the economy in the modern world. Both of these forces built upon the achievements of the scholastics, but took them in radical new directions. And, paradoxically, these two new forces held diametrically opposed worldviews.

Humanism developed two faces when it came to the question of God. The early humanists criticized the excesses of scholastic theology without taking any clear theological stands of their own. Eventually, however, humanism had to think about its own ultimate basis. Was the humanist movement attacking medieval theology in order to build a better theology that would be more faithful to God and his word? Or was it against theology across the board—against God?

The answer turned out to be "both." And the two faces of humanism were revealed in the same year. In 1517, Martin Luther posted his revolutionary Ninety-Five Theses, laying key theological groundwork for the Reformation. In the same year, Niccolo Machiavelli published his equally revolutionary *The Prince*, laying key philosophical groundwork for modern secularism. Both works were deeply informed by the best and latest humanist scholarship, and both were widely read throughout Europe, with consequences so vast that they continue to unfold around us today.

The religious crisis of the Reformation was also a political and economic crisis. First in Protestant domains, and later in Catholic domains, the urgent questions raised by the Reformation greatly accelerated the medieval movement toward reforming the world's economic practices in light of Christian moral commitments. At the same time, the crisis opened up much more radical possibilities for reform by unsettling old religious certainties. Both the Reformation and the Counter-Reformation—a set of aggressive reforms adopted by the Roman Catholic Church in response to the Reformation—demanded new and greater levels of economic change to bring about justice and mercy in the world. The era in which Christians go beyond advancing gradual economic reforms, but strive to rethink economics from the ground up in light of Christ and the Bible, began in the sixteenth century and has continued in unbroken succession through the present day.

Meanwhile, the sixteenth century also began the growth of modern secularism, with its exaltation of technological progress for its own sake and its suppression of moral questions in the public square. *The Prince* is a misunderstood and misrepresented book. Machiavelli himself was not really Machiavellian. He was no mere sycophant of scoundrels and tyrants, making excuses for any and all crimes powerful people wanted to commit. His goal was to rescue Italy from dire poverty and foreign oppression, because he cared about Italy deeply. He advocated reforms that he thought would benefit the people as well as the rulers, and bring back the classical glory and virtue of Italy in its pagan Roman heyday. However, the beating heart of *The Prince* is the idea that political and economic systems become irrational and dysfunctional if they rely on God as a guide to everyday life. Italy suffered dire poverty and foreign oppression, Machiavelli thought, because it had taken the Christian God too seriously. That is why he, notoriously, told rulers that they needed to be ready to do cruel and treacherous things when the public good demanded it. A few would be harmed, but the many would live and flourish.

Machiavelli was not the modern Pontius Pilate, annihilating all concern for justice by asking, insincerely, "What is truth?" That kind of secularism would not come until much later, in the nineteenth and twentieth centuries. Machiavelli was the modern Caia-phas, solemnly admonishing the Christian rulers of Italy that it is better that one man should die for the people than that the whole nation should perish.

The role of humanism's secular side in the development of the modern economy has been a subject of great debate. Scholars now widely recognize that an emphasis on scientific and technological development, by itself, was not the really important contribution.[14] The secularistic humanists did strongly emphasize natural science. But most large-scale civilizations, including medieval Europe under the scholastics, have practiced some kind of natural science, and some have made great scientific advances. Yet none even began to produce anything like the explosion of economic and technological growth in the modern economy.

A more important role played by the secular face of human-ism was connecting scientific progress to social progress. We use science to understand nature progressively better and better, and this increasing knowledge produces technical solutions to physi-cal problems. So why not use science to understand society pro-gressively better and better, producing technical solutions to social problems? It was thought that poverty and injustice could be solved by rational rulers and experts thinking through the right ways of reorganizing society. This demanded a rationalistic reevaluation of social order, suppressing moral questions (which are not scientific) in favor of social analysis as a technical science. In the modern secular view, a scientific society is not just a society that produces scientific progress, but a society that is itself produced by scientific progress—specifically, the science of social organization.

The development of this view can be traced in direct lines from Machiavelli through diverse thinkers such as Francis Bacon, Thomas Hobbes, David Hume, John Stuart Mill, Karl Marx, John

---

[14] See Deirdre McCloskey, *Bourgeois Dignity: Why Economics Can't Explain the Modern World* (Chicago: University of Chicago Press, 2010), 355–65.

Dewey, and John Rawls. The underlying assumption in all their works is that social problems arise largely from the superstitions of popular religion. This assumption is sometimes openly stated and sometimes prudently left unstated.

This line of thought played an essential role in the formation of modern economic thinking. In the Middle Ages, as we have seen, analysis of economic issues was a subset of moral philosophy. In the modern period, building on foundations laid by the secular side of humanism, economic thinking gradually detached itself from moral philosophy. The emergence of "economics" as a discipline during the Enlightenment represented an increased level of attention to economic issues, but also an attempt to think about economies in the same naturalistic way we think about the movements of molecules and stars.[15] This new science of economics would produce enormous new knowledge because of the increased attention given to economic issues, but it would also produce the secular economic ideologies we will look at in chapter 6.

A NEW WORLD EMERGES

All these developments contributed to a radically new world in two ways. One was the emergence, for the first time in world history, of sustained economic growth. Until the early modern period, the whole world lived at subsistence level, with barely enough wealth to keep body and soul together. The growth of commerce, the emergence of firms, the availability of money loans, and the acceleration of technological advancement brought about a radically new economic situation.

One of the main factors in that growth was the second of the two ways medieval economic development remade the world: the extension of greater dignity and rights to previously subordinated classes within Europe. As economic activity grew and developed,

---

[15] See Germano Maifreda, *From* Oikonomia *to Political Economy: Constructing Economic Knowledge from the Renaissance to the Scientific Revolution* (Farnham, Surrey, England: Ashgate, 2012).

increasing numbers of people devoted their professional lives to buying and selling, as opposed to the traditional lifestyles of farmers and craftsmen, for whom buying and selling was a necessary but secondary part of their daily lives. And the fruit of this emerging commercial class, which we now call the middle class or the bourgeois class, was not corruption and ruin. It was greater economic well-being for all. Christian leaders were increasingly forced to recognize the legitimacy of commerce, and grant dignity and social standing to economic professions previously considered intrinsically greedy and destructive. We will trace these two related developments—growth and the extension of social respect and rights—in the next chapter.

5

THE MODERN CRISIS

FROM STATIC TO DYNAMIC ECONOMICS

The modern world was created by the forces of medieval history we traced in the previous chapter—and yet, the modern world is also something radically new. Economic, political, and religious systems have been reinvented, often on principles directly opposed to those that prevailed throughout the world for all of recorded history. In the economic sphere, increased freedom for people outside the highest ranks of the elite to control their own work, property, and exchange has been accompanied by another phenomenon that was completely unforeseen: sustained economic growth, often at breathtaking rates. This new reality is both a cause and an effect of the broader changes in political, religious, and other kinds of social order in the modern world. In this new order, the pace and scope of social change is dramatically increased, bringing both unprecedented benefits and unprecedented challenges. Christian responses to these new conditions have played a key role in shaping this new economic world, as well as the life of the church itself.

ECONOMIC GROWTH CREATES A NEW WORLD

Significant and sustained economic growth is one of the most dramatic changes in human history. From the earliest known civilizations until relatively recently, the entire world experienced almost no sustained growth in levels of income. Of course, there were wealthy people, but the overwhelming majority lived at or near subsistence level (as we saw in chap. 3). The total amount of wealth usually didn't change. And in those rare cases where it did rise a bit for a while, such as in the heyday of the Roman Empire, before long it fell back to where it had been.[1]

At the height of the Middle Ages, as a result of the economic reforms we looked at in the previous chapter, modest rates of sustained economic growth began to happen in a few isolated localities in Europe. In the sixteenth century, this modest growth began spreading to more areas. Then, in the decades around 1800, the Industrial Revolution introduced rapidly accelerating growth that remade the face of England and the Netherlands, then Europe and North America, later Asia, and finally the entire world.[2]

A graph of income per person over the known course of history (Fig. 3.1) conveys the enormous scope of the change. A generation ago, it became common for economists to describe graphs like these as looking like hockey sticks, because they consisted of a long flat line with a sharp bend at the end. Lately, however, the exponential growth of the world's economies has become so extreme that the graphs look more like boomerangs—the growth of the last twenty years is so great that it creates a vertical line with a breathtaking ascent that rivals the unchanging horizontal stagnation of all preindustrial human history.

This growth is now happening in every part of the world, including Africa, Asia, and South America. Comfortable Westerners still tend to think of Africa as a continent of economic invalids, incapable of growth and permanently dependent upon foreign aid—which brings foreign political control and oppression—from nations with growing economies.[3] But the truth is that African nations *are* nations with growing economies. Of Africa's ten largest countries by population, nine experienced net economic growth between 1960

---

[1] See Angus Maddison, *Contours of the World Economy, 1–2030 AD: Essays in Macro-Economic History* (Oxford: Oxford University Press, 2007), 382, Table A.7.

[2] See Maddison, *Contours*, 382, Table A.7.

[3] Among the many books on how Western aid can be destructive to recipient countries, see for example Dambisa Moyo, *Dead Aid: Why Aid Is Not Working and How There Is a Better Way for Africa* (New York: Farrar, Straus and Giroux, 2010); and William Easterly, *The Tyranny of Experts: Economists, Dictators, and the Forgotten Rights of the Poor* (New York: Basic Books, 2015).

and 2011. Growth is occurring not only in relatively wealthy nations (South Africa, Algeria, and Egypt) but also in extremely poor nations (Ethiopia, Uganda, and Tanzania). Only the Democratic Republic of Congo, ravaged by civil war, is not growing.[4]

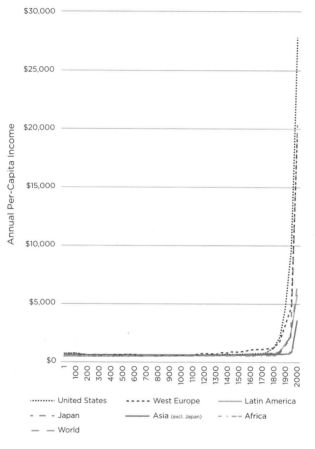

Fig. 5.1. Economic Growth, Globally and Regionally. (Data source: Angus Maddison, *Contours of the World Economy, 1–2030 AD: Essays in Macro-Economic History* [Oxford: Oxford University Press, 2007], 382.)

[4] See Greg Forster, "Opportunity: What Does Justice Require?" in *Economic Wisdom for Churches: A Primer on Poverty, Stewardship, and Flourishing,* ed. Adam Joyce and Greg Forster (Deerfield, IL: Oikonomia Network, 2017).

Growth has brought huge reductions in material poverty worldwide. As we noted in chapter 1, from 1970 to 2006, the number of people living on a dollar per day or less fell by 80 percent, while living standards more than doubled.[5]

But no Christian can ever think that material conditions matter more than moral conditions. Along with the material effects of growth come changes in social conditions, including both new moral triumphs and new moral calamities.

Technological progress and economic development are challenging traditional forms of social order, from politics to religion. Institutions in these areas don't function well in a world of dynamic growth because they were designed for a world of stable poverty. This has destroyed or undermined many oppressive and dysfunctional systems, and also many good and fruitful systems. The dictator and the pastor, the bonds of slavery and the bonds of community, racial segregation and sexual morality—all have difficulty maintaining their traditional places in a society where traditions are constantly upended by growth.

Technology and growth are also bringing all the world's nations and cultures into much more regular contact with one another through communication, trade, and migration. This global interconnectedness increases our opportunities for understanding and cooperation. It also increases our opportunities for resentment and conflict.

Moreover, the new instability and permeability of all our social boundaries has destabilized sources of identity and robbed cultural systems of meaning and purpose. This has made it harder to exclude people from equal social standing based on their ethnic background or religious beliefs. But it has also left people feeling disoriented and alienated, without stable sources of identity— a sense of chaos that sometimes feeds prejudice and extremism.

---

[5] Maxim Pinkovskiy and Xavier Sala-i-Martin, "Parametric Estimations of the World Distribution of Income," National Bureau of Economic Research, October 2009.

Mental-health problems are also increasing on numerous indicators; to take one example, the suicide rate for those under twenty-four increased 137 percent from 1950 to 1999.[6]

GROWTH CREATES A NEW WORLD BECAUSE IT WAS CREATED BY A NEW WORLD

Economies that grow over time are both the result and cause of a new kind of political and social order. The changes that brought about this transformation began to take on a much larger scale in the sixteenth century, building upon the earlier and more gradual achievements of the Middle Ages, as we saw in chapter 4. These changes, slowly at first but with increasing speed, undermined the older "natural" order we reviewed in chapter 3—what Douglass North and his coauthors called "the limited access order" because of its tight social control by a tiny elite class.

These new social forces reached their full effect from the late eighteenth to mid-nineteenth centuries, creating a new kind of political and social organization. North and his coauthors call this "the open access order." They write that the open-access order is characterized by:

1. A widely held set of beliefs about the inclusion of and equality for all citizens.
2. Unrestrained entry into economic, political, religious, and educational activities.
3. Support for organizational forms in each activity that is open to all (for example, contract enforcement).
4. Rule of law enforced impartially for all citizens.
5. Impersonal [economic] exchange [i.e., markets not limited to local communities].[7]

---

[6] Brian Fikkert and Michael Rhodes, "*Homo Economicus* Versus *Homo Imago Dei*," *Journal of Markets & Morality* 20, no. 1 (Spring 2017): 101–26.
[7] Douglass North, John Wallis, and Barry Weingast, *Violence and Social Orders: A Conceptual Framework for Interpreting Recorded Human History* (Cambridge: Cambridge University Press, 2009), 113.

Daily life in the open-access order is so dramatically different from the older kind of life that it's difficult even to realize how different it is. We can choose which religion to follow rather than facing oppression and death if we fail to believe everything our ancestors believed. We can elect those who govern us rather than being ruled by unaccountable monarchs and aristocrats. We can go into any line of work in which we can find a job instead of being required to spend our entire lives doing whatever kind of work our parents did. And we are free to choose whom we will marry and spend our lives with.

This massive social change required both of the "two faces of humanism" that we looked at in chapter 4, as well as the economic and technological growth sparked by medieval economic reform. We must resist the tendency to reduce the Industrial Revolution and the emergence of the modern world to a single cause. It is all too easy to say—and many people who are smart enough to know better have said it—that it was all exclusively the result of religious reform, and anything else that seems to have played a role was *really* just another area in which religious reform was causing change. Or that all the change was *really* a by-product of technological development, and anything else that appears to have been at work was just a product of the new technologies. Or that secular-scientific philosophy was the only engine of modernity, and all the religious fervor and technological upheaval of the age was *really* nothing more than the inevitable development of, and reactions to, the secular-scientific mind-set. In fact, the invention of the printing press and the development of cheaper systems for shipping goods (such as books) between cities, did not by itself create either the books of Martin Luther and his followers and detractors, or those of Niccolò Machiavelli and his followers and detractors; neither would those authors have reached the audiences they did without the invention of the printing press and cheaper shipping; neither did Luther make Machiavelli, nor Machiavelli Luther; and neither did religious reform alone nor secular reform alone suffice to invent modernity. You can't pull any of the threads out of this sweater without unraveling it. It is seamless, woven from the top throughout.

The Reformation and the Counter-Reformation both affirmed that the daily economic work of ordinary people is of immense importance to God. The doctrine of vocation arose to a new prominence in Christian thought. This is the teaching that all Christians' daily work in the ordinary economy represents a calling to glorify God as disciples of Jesus Christ by exercising love for God and neighbor through their work. During the Middle Ages, the idea of vocation had wrestled with an opposing idea, first championed by the early church figure Eusebius, that only the clergy were really advancing Christ's new life in the world through their daily activities. According to Eusebius, other people's daily work was morally legitimate, but they participated in the new life brought into the world by Christ only when they went to church and took part in clergy-led activities.[8] Although both ideas had their champions in the Middle Ages, Eusebius's ethical dualism usually had the upper hand. The Reformation and the Counter-Reformation inaugurated a new era of church history during which the doctrine of vocation has usually had the upper hand, especially among Protestants.

This increased religious respect for daily labor went hand in hand with an increased political respect for the people who did that labor. Protections for people's rights and freedoms were extended beyond the elite class for the first time. At first they were extended to the higher end of the middle class, or "bourgeoisie," which led the way in economic industrialization, and then further outward. Rights to vote, own property, and enjoy the protection of the rule of law were granted first to every male citizen of European descent who followed the right religion and owned land, then to every male citizen of European descent who owned land, then to every male citizen of European descent,

---

[8] See Edwin Woodruff Tait, "Duty and Delight," *Christian History* 110 (2014): 14–19.

then to every citizen of European descent, and finally to every citizen.

The secular face of humanism also contributed to the breaking down of the limited-access order and the emergence of the open-access order. Its most important contribution was to modern scientific thinking and technological progress. While every large civilization has had natural science, the scientific enterprise was generally carried out under the careful censorship of religious and political authorities. Moreover, scientific advances were not widely viewed as potential sources of practical technological innovation that could be harnessed to carry out an ambitious reshaping of daily life. The modern scientific and technological project—experimental method freed from arbitrary metaphysical dogma, and its findings systematically applied to practical problems—was largely developed as an outgrowth of the secular side of humanism.

Not all of the champions of modern science were themselves religious skeptics. Quite the contrary, many were very pious. And, of course, humanism itself was originally building upon the achievements of medieval scholasticism. The belief that the natural world is rational, upon which the scientific project relies and which the scientific project therefore cannot prove, is borrowed from Christianity with its rational God. The belief that the human mind can understand and control nature, upon which the scientific project relies and which the scientific project therefore cannot prove, is borrowed from Christianity with its view that humans are made in God's image. The belief that the power to understand and control nature ought to be used to improve the world, upon which the scientific project relies and which the scientific project therefore cannot prove, is borrowed from Christianity with its view that humans were made to be good stewards of God's world. The secular face of humanism was, and still is, not so much a rival to Christianity as a depraved parody of it—Christian thought chopped up and sewn back together, but with a giant God-shaped hole in the middle.

Nonetheless, the intellectual and moral resources of Christianity were never deployed in anything like the modern scientific project until the secular branch of humanism organized that project. The medieval scholars and Christian humanists were, in their different ways, interested in reforming society and improving the lot of the poor. But neither group originally put the advance of natural science and its resulting technological applications at the center of their ambitions for social improvement. Only after the secular side of humanism pursued that avenue of reform and proved that it had great power did organized Christian thought and leadership began to embrace it.

Both faces of humanism—religious reform and secular reform—contributed to economic growth and technological progress. Growth and technology, in turn, provided the necessary conditions for further religious and secular reform. The pace of change is constantly increasing, because every change that emerges increases both our desire to change the world (in the name of our religious and secular causes) and our power to change it. Change begets change begets change—and only God knows where it's all headed.

BRAVE NEW WORLD

The benefits of the open-access order are considerable. The collapse of global poverty rates and a corresponding increase in life expectancy are only the most obvious benefits—the material benefits. The advance toward universal respect for human dignity, while more subtle, is ultimately more significant. There was no place under the limited-access order for religious freedom, constitutional democracy, an equal public role for women, or respect for rights of work, property, and exchange under the rule of law. We can talk about a possible return to the limited-access order only if we are prepared to go back to enforced religious conformity, arbitrary rule, confinement of women to the home in arranged marriages, and the ordering of all economic affairs for the benefit of the powerful. But if we are committed to equal rights and freedoms in religion, politics, the family, and economics, we are committed to the open-access order.

However, economic growth and the open-access order also come with high social costs, and we must acknowledge and bear those costs if we want to keep our equal rights and freedoms. We cannot eat our cake and have it too. Giving people the right to control their own lives and make their own choices means living in a chaotic and unstable social environment. Economic growth means people have more power to do what they want, including things they shouldn't want. The potential catastrophe to which this emerging world could lead us was unforgettably illustrated in Aldous Huxley's novel *Brave New World*, the title of which suggests the foolish hubris of those who see no danger in the growth of choice and power without an accompanying growth in spiritual maturity.

Economic poverty is turning out to be stubbornly persistent, in spite of ongoing economic growth. In some ways, it is growing worse rather than better. It isn't that the material conditions of the economically poor have not improved. On the contrary, as the data cited above show, the economically poor have seen their material conditions improve dramatically. Poor people today have material standards of living well above those of middle-class people even a hundred years ago. Consider that in 1900, only one-quarter of U.S. households had running water, only one-twelfth had gas or electric lights, only one-twentieth had a telephone, and only one out of every ninety had a car—to say nothing of all the technologies and comforts we enjoy today that hadn't even been invented yet.[9] However, poverty is not primarily a lack of material resources. Poverty is primarily a lack of rightly ordered social relationships—family, work, and neighborhood relationships. And the chaotic social environment of the advanced modern world has been hardest on

---

[9] See Derek Thompson, "How America Spends Money," *The Atlantic*, April 5, 2012.

those who are least equipped to handle it. Divorce, illegitimacy, dropout rates, drug use, crime, and other social disorders are not functions of material wealth but of disordered social worlds, and it is among the economically poor that social worlds are most disordered. The economically poor have never had more material wealth, but their social condition has not necessarily improved. And many efforts to help the economically poor, whether through government, churches, or charities, are based on a belief that their needs are primarily material rather than relational. As a result, we often do more harm than good, increasing their dependence on us and our charity rather than increasing their independence and equal standing in the community.[10]

The legacy of racism, slavery, segregation, and colonialism is also still very much with us. Just as increasing material wealth does not get rid of poverty, it also does not remove the inequalities caused by these past and present injustices. As with poverty, the most important inequality here is not unequal distribution of material resources but unequal distribution of social resources—relationships, networks, and participation in social institutions. And as with poverty, the instability of social systems in the modern world makes the problem all the harder to cope with.

Historic Christianity and the secular side of humanism are both implicated in this legacy. In the late Middle Ages and early modernity, colonialism and slavery were justified on religious grounds—the Christians of Europe were held to have power over non-Christian populations because of their faith. This idea was never actually compatible with the official political theology and philosophy of Christian Europe, but there was enormous money and power to be had in exploiting foreign populations, so the niceties were not observed. Later, as the theological implausibility of religious justifications for colonialism and slavery became clear,

---

[10] See Steve Corbett and Brian Fikkert, *When Helping Hurts: How to Alleviate Poverty without Hurting the Poor . . . and Yourself* (Chicago: Moody Press, 2009).

secular-scientific theories of superior and inferior races became the justification.[11]

Another major challenge for modern economies is our lack of shared moral commitments. Many major economic dysfunctions in the modern world occur because respecting people's rights and freedoms, especially religious freedom, leaves society unable to enforce (legally or socially) high moral expectations. Results include catastrophic levels of debt, including household and government debt, because people want to get the benefits of spending money without paying the costs; a crisis of business ethics, in which people feel less and less confident they can trust the firms they work for and do business with every day not to swindle them; and cronyism, in which the elite use their access to power to rig the economic system in their own favor (a throwback to the ways of the limited-access order).

The lack of deep and strong shared moral commitments, in addition to being a problem in its own right, also leaves society less able to mobilize social responses to other kinds of challenges. The opening of freer international trade and communication, commonly called *globalization*, disrupts settled ways of life and forces some people out of their jobs. If we had a stronger moral culture, we would mobilize to alleviate those disruptions much more than we do. Technological and economic development create greater economic inequality because they allow those with especially valuable natural gifts or social opportunities to mobilize and monetize their advantages much more efficiently. In a morally strong culture, the mere possession of unequal amounts of money probably would not create a social crisis, because we would have confidence that those who had more money than we do (1) had legitimately earned what they have, rather than gaining it by gaming the system, and (2) would use it in morally good ways—and if they didn't, we would be ready to call them out for it. As it is, however, our lack

---

[11] See George Fredrickson, *Racism: A Short History* (Princeton, NJ: Princeton University Press, 2015).

of moral solidarity leaves us feeling as if the rich didn't really earn what they have and can get away with using it selfishly.

Perhaps the most destructive and perplexing challenge of the open-access order and its accompanying economic growth is the breakdown of the family, the church, and other key social institutions. These breakdowns are increasingly recognized as a key factor in social problems ranging from poverty and crime to mental illness and suicide to political polarization and extremism. One reason these institutions are profoundly challenged in the open-access order is moral fragmentation—in an environment of religious freedom, there is less general agreement about what is good and right, and as a result, it is difficult to maintain a social consensus that we must make the painful sacrifices in our lives necessary to sustain institutions such as the family and the church.

However, another factor is more directly economic. People who have more wealth can more easily escape painful social obligations. In the older world, a man who scandalously betrayed his wife and children would face social opprobrium for the rest of his life. In our rich and mobile society, he can simply move away and start again. In the older world, when the overwhelming majority of the population lived within clear sight of starvation level, and a single war, famine, or natural disaster could ruin everyone, people felt a need to stay within religious communities that established mutual obligation. In our rich and comfortable society, people do not feel themselves to be constantly under threat of death from unexpected misfortune, so they feel less need to make sacrifices to keep themselves in good standing with social communities whose aid they might need.

CHRIST'S BRAVE NEW WORLD

Christian responses to these new challenges and opportunities have played a key role in reshaping this new social and economic order as it has emerged. The church has felt itself obligated to speak and act within the open-access order. That is partly because the holy love of God demands our participation in the life of our communities for the sake of our neighbors. And it is partly because we ourselves cannot live as disciples of Jesus if our participation in economic systems, which is such a pervasive part of our lives, does not manifest the new life we have in Christ. And as Christians have taken the initiative to speak and live in Christlike ways in the modern economy, these things have not been done in a corner.

As farm life gave way to factory life, early factories were unsanitary and inhumane. Factory towns were rampant with alcoholism and despair. It was Christians who took the lead in opposing child factory labor, demanding sanitation and other human services, and reforming the factory. It was also Christians who took the lead in confronting the workers in factory towns about addiction and apathy, insisting they show up at their jobs sober, work hard, and do their jobs with excellence.

The growing wealth and power of European and American nations greatly increased their capacity to exploit the riches and enslave the labor of other populations. The Industrial Revolution brought with it the rise of what might be called an *international Slave-Industrial Complex*. It was Christians who took the lead in confronting and dismantling these economic injustices in the nineteenth and twentieth centuries.

If we choose, we can use our freedom to make a brave new world of materialistic individualism. But that supposedly brave new world is really a cowardly old world. It is the spiritually dead world of cold egoism and cosmic despair—the same world of fear and greed that created and sustained the limited-access order for most of human history. It will drag us back there if we let it.

Christ also has a brave new world—one that is really brave and really new. It is the brave new world of redemption and restoration through the cross and the empty tomb. It is really new because it overturns the dominion of fear and greed. It is really brave because it leads us out of our familiar Egypts and Babylons into a wilderness, going we know not where (but he does). When Christ returns, he will destroy the brave new world of materialistic hubris and consummate his own brave new world of God's holy love.

Today, by the Holy Spirit, spreading the gospel and building up a people who live out the holy love of God they have received in Christ, God is bringing a preview of his brave new world into the present. In the next chapter, we will look at some specific ways we can escape materialistic economics and express the holy love of God in economic life.

6

ECONOMIC IDOLS AND ECONOMIC WISDOM

FROM IDEOLOGICAL CAPTIVITY TO THEOLOGICAL TRANSFORMATION

Our world is dominated by the idolatrous worship of economic ideologies. Theological understanding has given way to more secular explanations of economic matters that exclude the supernatural. Like all worldly ideologies, these have taken a variety of forms. Some people's prejudices and interests lead them to hold one ideology, while other people with different prejudices and interests hold another. Each of these worldly ideological systems has some good insights—after all, if they didn't get at least some things right, they wouldn't attract many followers. Yet they all fall short in critical ways because they cannot sufficiently escape worldly prejudices and interests. For their devoted followers, these ideologies offer up substitutes, created by human hands, to replace the presence and provision of God as the ultimate source of our flourishing and hope.

We would be naive to think that we, as Christians, have nothing to do with the idolatry of worldly economic ideologies. On the contrary, the thinking and behavior of Christians today is all too deeply captive to the world's economic idols. Christians are supposed to be transformed by the renewing of our minds, not conformed to the world. Living out the holy love of God, manifesting the new life we have in Christ in our daily lives, and helping create a preview of the brave new world Christ will consummate when he returns require us to rethink the economic assumptions we have inherited from the futile ways of our fathers (1 Pet. 1:18).

However, we would be equally naive to think that we can totally repudiate existing systems of economic thought and set up "Christian economics" against them. That is not how the Holy Spirit works. At Pentecost, the people of many nations did not hear the gospel preached in a totally new language. They heard it in their own languages, the existing languages of human culture. God does not remove us from cultural systems—which include systems of economic thinking—when he redeems us. Rather, he creates new life within our hearts that we manifest outwardly by building new ways of life within the cultural systems of our nations. We cannot escape the sins of our nations by building a wall around the church, for we ourselves are members of our nations, formed by their cultures and systems. Inside the wall we build around the church, we will find the same sins we found on the outside, only now they will have Jesus fish symbols and Bible verses pasted all over them.

Believers must find new ways of participating in the modern economy as people who are part of our communities and their economic systems, but who have found a new life that changes everything for us. This must involve finding new ways of thinking about the modern economy, and that means challenging the idols of economic ideologies. But as we challenge the idolatry of these ideologies, we should begin by lovingly affirming what is right in them and showing genuine concern for the real and serious problems that often motivate the people who create them. Only then, challenging idolatry from the position of active and loving participation in the economic life and thinking of our communities, will we be living out holy love and not the arrogance of self-righteous Pharisaism.

LEGITIMATE CONCERN FOR THE
INTEGRITY OF MARKETS

One good thing that often becomes an idol is "the market," meaning systems in which buyers and sellers, protected by law against theft, force, and fraud, exchange things at prices they freely agree on. In the United States, idolatry of the market is the primary spiritual danger facing those who belong to the movements known as "conservative" and "libertarian." Elsewhere, it is those known as "liberal" or "neoliberal" who are most in this danger.

There is a legitimate need to protect markets from unjust and arbitrary interference. The danger is not caring about markets. The danger is trusting in markets rather than God as the ultimate source of our economic well-being.

Concern to protect markets usually comes from a legitimate starting point. There are many needs and problems in daily life for which the role of markets is indispensable. People generally benefit one another when they engage in voluntary exchange. While some voluntary market exchanges are bad (the purchase of drugs or pornography, for example), the overwhelming majority of the buying and selling that happens every day is good and necessary. Interfering with the market even in seemingly small ways can create widespread disruption. Through voluntary exchange, markets set prices that reveal critical information about supply and demand. Higher prices mean demand is up, supply is down, or both; lower prices mean the opposite. This information, which only a freely operating market can discover, is critical to people making good choices about how they manage resources, specialize their work, and exchange with others in daily life. When people do not control their own daily economic choices, the price system cannot provide accurate information about supply and demand, and people don't know how to manage resources, specialize work, or exchange efficiently.[1]

---

[1] See Victor V. Claar and Robin J. Klay, *Economics in Christian Perspective: Theory, Policy, and Life Choices* (Downers Grove, IL: InterVarsity Press, 2007), 28–48; and Brent Waters, *Just*

Concern for markets can also begin from a legitimate reaction against idolatry of the state, which we will look at further below. Confronted with severe economic problems such as poverty, or even with the discomfort created by the normal ups and downs of economic cycles, there is a temptation to try to solve these problems by giving government arbitrary power to change market outcomes. But giving government the power to overrule market outcomes by direct fiat always involves giving powerful people—politicians and their cronies—unaccountable control over other people's lives. Control of economic life affects people at a very intimate level. Such power is inevitably abused for the benefit of the powerful, because the whole idea of giving this power to government begins with the negation of the dignity of human beings as responsible stewards who have a mandate from God to manage their own corner of God's world.[2]

Any serious approach to economics must include an appreciation for the role price systems play in providing vital information about supply and demand. Moreover, as Christianity holds that human beings are made to be stewards of the world together, Christians ought to appreciate the importance of respecting people's rights and freedoms—treating all people as fellow stewards rather than giving some people arbitrary power over others to control their stewardship. And Christians also ought to appreciate the role of market exchange as a medium through which people can steward the world *together* by exchanging their gifts.

THE AUTONOMOUS MARKET AS IDOL

Alas, it is all too easy—and all too commonplace—to leap to the conclusion that the market is sufficient, by itself, to solve our problems for us without God. People who are disconnected from the Christian account of reality, or who have not thought through its implications carefully, often view the market as an automatically

---

Capitalism: A Christian Ethic of Economic Globalization (Louisville: Westminster John Knox, 2016), 40–59.

[2] See Whittaker Chambers, *Witness* (Washington, DC: Regnery, 1952), xxxiii–1, 153–60, 385–88.

self-correcting system. Whatever problems we have, we only have to let the market function and find a solution. All of us have encountered the free-market zealot who responds to any economic question by starting with the conclusion that a freer market is all we need to solve the problem, and then reasons backward from that conclusion to construct an argument for why freer markets are the solution. It seems that markets will solve any problem for us (except theft, force, or fraud) if we just get out of the way.

This sets up the market as an autonomous force independent of God. Borrowing T. S. Eliot's famous language, idolaters of markets "constantly try to escape / From the darkness outside and within / By dreaming of systems so perfect that no one will need to be good."[3] Different ideologies account for the autonomy of the market in different ways. Some hold that human beings pursuing their own natural, rational self-interest—without a transcendent, supernatural source of moral virtue—are enough not only to sustain markets but to make the market a self-contained engine of social progress. Others subscribe to a more extreme narrative in which individuals, or some individuals, are radically free and self-created, making choices with a godlike capacity to transcend the limitations of history, culture, family, or (above all) moral defects in the human heart. These quasidivine entrepreneurs invent the economic and social world from their inward, autonomous resources of creative power. Either way, for its idolaters, the market operates by the equivalent of natural laws, requiring no basis in transcendent moral and metaphysical commitments, and no ties of community. The economy hums along fine without God, depending on the rational self-interest of human nature or the transcendent power of godlike entrepreneurs to ensure problems are corrected.

A good look around us in the advanced modern world should be enough to convince us that economic growth and flourishing

---

[3] T. S. Eliot, "Choruses from 'The Rock,'" in *Collected Poems: 1909–1962* (New York: Harcourt Brace Jovanovich, 1991), 160.

are not sustainable in the long term without God. The open-access order and its accompanying economic growth create a social environment in which churches, families, and other critical social structures find it harder and harder to play their roles. As people become detached from these social institutions, they become selfishly individualistic and lose the moral virtues (honesty, diligence, generosity) needed to sustain a market economy. Societies in which we primarily relate to strangers through economic relationships, in which we are not held together by a shared religion or any other comprehensive metaphysical or philosophical account of the cosmos, also tend to break down in moral fragmentation and polarization. Popular reactions against market economies, whether they take the form of left-wing socialism or right-wing nationalism, are primarily produced by this atomized and polarized social environment. While the open-access order and market economies may be preferable to the available alternatives, it is clear that they also create new challenges that cannot be solved simply by doubling down on free markets over and over again.

Of course, it is true that the image of God remains in sinful human beings, so every society is able to sustain some sort of economy, with or without God. But what kinds of economies are sustainable without God? Not the growing and dynamic economies of modernity, but the static and oppressive economies of the limited-access order. Affirmations of equal human dignity and human rights, which came with the rise of Christianity, were indispensable elements in the emergence of the open-access order, with its social liberation and economic growth. And equal human dignity and human rights would not continue long without the open-access order.

This implies that our appreciation for markets must be tempered by an awareness of their limitations, and especially their dependence on moral principles that have transcendent sources. The market must bend to morality, a morality that demands concern for the flourishing of the poor and marginalized, rather than morality to the market. And we must rely on God rather than on the market as the real solution to our problems. The market is a place where Christians can make godly choices and create solutions to social problems, and they have very often done so. But it is that godliness, not the market, that creates the solutions.

Christians who are not themselves highly influenced by free-market movements should take time to understand, in a sympathetic way, why so many of their brothers and sisters in Christ feel such an urgent need to protect markets from arbitrary interference. At the same time, Christians who are highly influenced by free-market movements have a special obligation to resist idolatry of the market. It is those Christians above all who should be at the forefront of affirming that the market depends on transcendent moral standards and must submit to those standards—and that there are no adequate and sustainable solutions to economic problems without the supernatural presence and provision of God in Jesus Christ.

LEGITIMATE CONCERN FOR MODIFYING MARKETS

A second good thing that often becomes an idol is political intervention in market systems to advance justice and human flourishing. This intervention takes many forms, including direct redistribution of wealth through transfer payments, mandates requiring businesses and others to provide specific resources and services, and government-run systems that provide specific resources and services directly to those who need them. Idolizing such intervention is the primary spiritual danger facing those on the progressive/globalist left and those on the populist/nationalist right. It is a danger not only among those who take extreme views that exalt the state to totalitarian control, as in fascism and communism. This idolatry also comes in softer and more immediately attractive forms, which are less violent and hateful but ultimately still lead people away from dependence on God and into dependence on the state.

There is a legitimate need to modify markets to accommodate the needs of justice and mercy. The danger is not modifying markets. The danger is trusting in such interventions rather than God as the ultimate source of our economic well-being.

Concern to modify markets usually comes from a legitimate starting point. One is concern about the legacy of historic injustices against ethnic minorities and others, the long-term effects of which continue to be visible in market outcomes. The moral legitimacy of market systems depends on the presupposition that when people have been wronged, those wrongs will be redressed. Historic injustices are not fully remedied by antidiscrimination laws. Even if all invidious discrimination had ceased in the present—which it has not—we would still inherit a world profoundly distorted by the invidious discrimination of the past. It is true that the individuals alive today are not culpable for crimes committed before we were born. However, while we are not culpable for what was done, we are nonetheless responsible to redress the consequences. We are the inheritors of the social order that committed these historic injustices, so we are responsible to clean up the mess our ancestors bequeathed to us.

Concern to modify markets can also begin from a legitimate doubt that charitable giving among churches and other community groups is sufficient to care for the needs of the economically poor. It is true that churches should lead the way in taking care of the poor. If God's people were as generous as they should be, churches would be doing so much for the poor that government's role would become secondary. And it is true that before the rise of the open-access order in the modern world, charity was primarily a responsibility of religious institutions or wealthy patrons rather than government. However, this does not imply government had no role in charity. At that time, religious and civic authorities were heavily interdependent on one another's authority, so they always cooperated. A destitute man in medieval times would be taken in by the church, but the church would feed him using revenue it collected with the implicit, and often explicit, involvement of civil law and political power. Moreover, in the morally fragmented culture created by the open-access order, it would be naive to think that voluntary charitable giving through churches and other community organizations would automatically reach levels high enough to meet our needs. There is no doubt that if we abolished all welfare-state programs overnight, church and private giving would rise in response to this sudden gap in resources. But in the chaotic and disjointed cultures of the modern world, it is unrealistic to expect it would rise at a one-for-one rate to match the sudden disappearance of government aid. Finally, part of the challenge of poverty in the modern world is precisely the lack of social capital—relationships—that would connect people in need to the churches and community organizations that ideally would be the ones to help them.

Any serious approach to economics must include an appreciation for the role political systems play in ensuring that at least the most basic needs of justice and mercy are met. Moreover, as Christianity holds that God has a special concern for those who are impoverished or marginalized, Christians ought to appreciate the importance of ensuring that legitimate concern for the integrity of economic systems does not simply override and negate the equally legitimate concern for the flourishing of those most in need. And they ought to appreciate that doing justice and mercy in a fallen world is not a simple matter that can be carried out by abstract formulas.

THE AUTONOMOUS STATE AS IDOL

Alas, it is all too easy—and all too commonplace—to leap to the conclusion that government intervention in the market is sufficient, by itself, to solve our problems for us without God. People who are disconnected from the Christian account of reality, or who have not thought through its implications carefully, often view government as an automatically self-correcting system. Whatever problems we have, we only have to let government function and find a solution. All of us have encountered the welfare-state zealot who responds to any economic question by starting with the conclusion that bigger government programs are all we need to solve the problem, and then reasons backward from that conclusion to construct an argument for why government is the solution. It seems the government will solve any problem for us if we just give it more money and power.

This sets up government as an autonomous force independent of God. Like the idolaters of the autonomous market, idolaters of the autonomous state "constantly try to escape / From the darkness outside and within / By dreaming of systems so perfect that no one will need to be good."[4] Different ideologies account for the autonomy of government in different ways. Some treat human needs as merely material and not spiritual, as if we could live by bread alone. This materialistic view implies that we can create justice and solve our economic problems simply by moving money around. This requires giving effectively unlimited power to a tiny class of rational, technocratic experts who can figure out which money needs to be moved where. Others have an excessive investment in protecting traditional ethnic, religious, or other social identities against the cultural chaos of the open-access order. From this point of view, every economic problem becomes an example of how "they" (immigrants, blacks, Jews, Catholics, the Chinese, the Russians, secular humanists, evangelicals—every Emmanuel Goldstein imaginable) are out to get "us," so the power of government—which, of course, rightfully belongs to "us" and has been corrupted or usurped by "them"—should intervene in the market to protect "us" from "them." Either way, for its idolaters, interventionist government is always presumptively pure, good, and right, requiring no basis in transcendent moral and metaphysical com-

---

[4] Eliot, "Choruses," 160.

mitments, and no protections for individual rights and freedoms to ensure that the ties of community remain authentic and humane. Government hums along fine without God, depending on rational expertise or ethnic/religious/cultural homogeneity to ensure problems are corrected.

A good look around us in the advanced modern world should be enough to convince us that solutions to injustice and poverty are not sustainable in the long term without God. Large expansions of government programs designed to fight poverty have improved the material conditions of the poor, but have not produced significant reductions in poverty itself. We have made discouragingly little sustained headway on the problem of long-term dependency of the poor upon indiscriminate one-way giving by government programs. Meanwhile, populist/nationalist schemes to use government power to exclude outsiders from economic participation in order to increase the solidarity of the community—tariffs, immigration restrictions, "buy American" and "hire American" incentives, public attacks by powerful politicians against companies that supposedly lack "economic patriotism"—have an even worse track record. The moral fragmentation of community under the conditions of the open-access order and market economies is a real problem. But populist/nationalist use of government power, far from solving that problem, only inflames existing divisions and creates ongoing political incentives to maintain and deepen them.

Of course, it is true that the image of God remains in sinful human beings, so every society is able to sustain some sort of government system, with or without God. But what kind of governments are sustainable without God? Not modern regimes affirming equality and freedom, but the brutally hierarchical and authoritarian regimes of the limited-access order. Affirmation of equal justice for the marginalized and genuine concern for the impoverished, which came with the rise of Christianity, were indispensable elements in the emergence of the open-access order, with its social liberation and economic growth. And justice for the marginalized and concern for the impoverished would not continue long without the open-access order.

This implies that our appreciation for government must be tempered by an awareness of its limitations, and especially its dependence on moral principles that have transcendent sources. Political systems must bend to morality, a morality that demands respect for the rights and freedoms of individuals, rather than morality to political systems. And we must rely on God rather than on government as the real solution to our problems. Politics is a domain in which Christians can make godly choices and create solutions to social problems, and they have very often done so. But it is that godliness, not the government, that creates the solutions.

Christians who are not themselves highly influenced by progressive or populist movements should take time to understand, in a sympathetic way, why so many of their brothers and sisters in Christ feel such an urgent need for government programs that go beyond protections against theft, force, and fraud. At the same time, Christians who are highly influenced by progressive or populist movements have a special obligation to resist idolatry of the state. It is those Christians above all who should be at the forefront of affirming that the state depends on transcendent moral standards and must submit to those standards—and that there are no adequate and sustainable solutions to economic problems without the supernatural presence and provision of God in Jesus Christ.

SEEKING ECONOMIC WISDOM

Overcoming these idolatries is the work of the coming generation. It will require a willingness to look past ideological formulas and polarized group loyalties. This is not likely to work if it means setting up a "Christian economics" that stands against other systems. The way of the Holy Spirit is to transform and perfect existing cultural structures rather than to discard and replace them. When we forget this, we reduce Christianity to one more combatant in the endless culture wars.

Economic wisdom will, however, involve a distinct Christian economic life, preached and practiced by God's people both in their churches and in their professions out in the world. Pulpits must preach a gospel that speaks to all of life, including the part of life that people spend most of their waking hours participating in and not just the tiny sliver of life they spend in church. This includes not just personal holiness but insight about systemic arrangements and a witness against the evil and injustice of worldly powers. Then, on the other six days, the people of God must organize to build an economic life that practices the wisdom of God in Christ, brings flourishing to the community, and pushes back against the power of evil.

It will also involve distinct Christian ways of processing economic questions and disputes. In societies paralyzed by polarization, Christians must become the people who are able to listen to one another across partisan and ideological divides. This is part of what it means to tear down the dividing walls of cultural opposition among those who are united in Christ and called to live together as God's people. Like Jews and Gentiles learning to live in community in the New Testament, the capacity of God's people to own one another's concerns and find ways to move forward together—even in the midst of the disagreements we will no doubt continue to have—will be a powerful evidence of the reality of the Holy Spirit's work.

Over time, such approaches would develop into a "Christian economics" in a different sense—one that brings life to the world rather than bringing it yet another battle in the culture war. Christ continues the holy war to reclaim God's creation order by redeeming us through his Spirit to live as good stewards of that creation order. His brave new world of holy love in the kingdom of God challenged, and ultimately helped to destroy, the cowardly old world of the limited-access order. Today, Christ's authentic brave new world challenges the phony brave new worlds of materialistic worldliness that have risen to power in the open-access order—the economic idolatries of autonomous markets and states.

By faith, we know that Christ's is the real brave new world, the traumatic inauguration of a radical new reality. Its full coming, when it arrives, will usher in an eternity of justice, peace, mercy, and flourishing, with a beauty and joy that will surpass all our present dim glimpses of it as dramatically as the summer sunshine surpasses a pinprick of light in a dark room. Our job is to make that pinprick a little bit wider every day. By God's grace, millions of Christians are already doing just that. It is a high and holy calling that we receive afresh each Sunday and carry into every domain of work and economic exchange on the other six days of the week.

QUESTIONS FOR REFLECTION

1. In what specific ways did you rely on other people to do their work today? How many people were involved?

2. How is the gospel of Christ important for the way people do their daily work? How is it important for the way they buy and sell? (Try to go beyond basic ethical requirements such as not lying and stealing.)

3. What economic systems and practices are you aware of that prevent all people from having equal access to participate in the economy? What systems and practices expand opportunity?

4. How is the idea of human rights related to Christian doctrine? What rights are important for our daily economic lives and for the larger flourishing of our economies?

5. What are the important, legitimate economic concerns you hear from the political left and right, and what do you hear from each that needs to be challenged? How many responsible, worthwhile voices do you listen to from perspectives opposite to your own, and how charitably do you listen?

GLOSSARY

Division of Labor. See *Specialization.*

Economics. The academic discipline that studies the economy.

Economy. In a strict sense of the term, an economy is a social system for exchanging work and the fruits of work, allowing individuals and organizations to specialize (see *Specialization*); in a broader sense, it is the whole human community of interdependence.

Globalization. A historical trend in which economies of separate nations are becoming more interdependent through improved communication and transportation technologies, and the lowering of legal and cultural barriers to economic exchange.

Homo Economicus. A model of human economic behavior widely used among economists that assumes God is irrelevant to happiness, people have autonomous consumption-oriented desires, and people are by nature one another's rivals because their autonomous consumption desires conflict.

Industrial Revolution. A historical development approximately two hundred years ago that introduced sustained and increasing economic growth for the first time, allowing us to live above the subsistence-level poverty that had been the universal human experience before.

Money. A medium of exchange that allows people to trade the value of their work more efficiently.

Specialization. A natural tendency in all economies by which people and organizations invest most of their work hours in one kind (or a few kinds) of work that others value from them most.

Stewardship. Humanity's God-given responsibility to cultivate and protect the world, a core feature of the image of God in human beings.

RESOURCES FOR FURTHER STUDY

"A Christian Vision for Flourishing Communities," Oikonomia Network, https://oikonomianetwork.org/wp-content/uploads/2016/07/Christian-Vision-for-Flourishing-Communities.pdf.

Blomberg, Craig. *Neither Poverty nor Riches: A Biblical Theology of Possessions.* Downers Grove, IL: InterVarsity Press, 2000.

Claar, Victor V., and Robin J. Klay. *Economics in Christian Perspective: Theory, Policy, and Life Choices.* Downers Grove, IL: InterVarsity Press, 2007.

Corbett, Steve, and Brian Fikkert. *When Helping Hurts: How to Alleviate Poverty without Hurting the Poor . . . and Yourself.* Chicago: Moody Publishers, 2014.

Grudem, Wayne. *Business for the Glory of God: The Bible's Teaching on the Moral Goodness of Business.* Wheaton, IL: Crossway, 2003.

Joyce, Adam, and Greg Forster, eds. *Economic Wisdom for Churches: A Primer on Poverty, Stewardship, and Flourishing.* Deerfield, IL: Oikonomia Network, 2017.

Nelson, Tom. *The Economics of Neighborly Love: Investing in Your Community's Compassion and Capacity.* Downers Grove, IL: InterVarsity Press, 2017.

Sherman, Amy L. *Kingdom Calling: Vocational Stewardship for the Common Good.* Downers Grove, IL: InterVarsity Press, 2011.

Waters, Brent. *Just Capitalism: A Christian Ethic of Economic Globalization.* Louisville: Westminster John Knox, 2016.

Willard, Dallas, and Gary Black Jr. *The Divine Conspiracy Continued: Fulfilling God's Kingdom on Earth.* New York: HarperOne, 2015.

GENERAL INDEX

Adam, 27, 29, 35, 36–37, 48
Africa, 84–85, 85 f5.1
Algeria, 85
Aquinas, Thomas, 17, 68, 70, 71, 72
Aristotle, 60, 70
Asia, 85f5.1
Augustine, 17, 58
authoritarian system, 59
autonomous consumption desires,
    26, 30–31

Bacon, Francis, 79
Boaz, 39, 47
bourgeois class. *See* middle class
Brave New World (Huxley), 92
business ethics, 94
buying and selling, 22–23, 57, 69–70,
    72, 81, 101

capitalism, 76
charitable giving, 106–7
China, 25
Christianity, 90–91, 93–94
Christians: blind spots of early,
    63–65; daily work of, 89; eco-
    nomic idolatry of, 99–100; free
    markets and, 105; identity of, 63;
    open access order and, 95–96;
    politics and, 110; questioning the
    economy by, 67; role in society
    of, 100; work and, 62
church, the: breakdown of, 95; di-
    versity in, 46; early concerns of,
    73; early ideals in, 61–63; instruc-

tions for life by, 42–43; mission
    of, 43, 45; moral philosophy and,
    68; purpose of, 44; the world
    and, 52
colonialism, 75–76, 93
commerce, 70
commercial class. *See* middle class
community, 37
companionship, 37
compassion, 51–52
cooperation, 36–37
Counter-Reformation, 78, 89
creation, 28, 35–36
cronyism, 94
cultivating, 28
curse, of the fall, 37–38

Daniel, 57
debt, 94
Dewey, John, 79–80
disciples, living as, 47
discipleship, 44
diversity, 46
The Divine Conspiracy (Willard), 49

economy, the: ancient, 56–57; cor-
    ruption of, 32; defined, 18–19;
    early Christians within, 63–65;
    industrial, 48; land-based, 48;
    measurement of, 29–30; theologi-
    cal perspective of, 27–31
Egypt, 85
Eliot, T. S., 103
elites, 55–56

Enlightenment, 80
Ethiopia, 85
Europe, 73, 74, 84, 85f5.1
Eve, 27, 29, 35, 48
exchange: act of, 30; defined, 22–25; forms of, 69; Golden Rule within, 71; justice within, 69–72; power of, 25; unjust, 71–72; voluntary, 101; working as, 37
exploitation, 41–42, 71

factories, 96
fall, the, 31, 37, 54
family, 95
farming, 56
Fikkert, Brian, 26
freedom, 24, 32
free markets, 103, 105
fruitfulness, 50
fruit of the Spirit, 50

generosity: act of, 39; Jesus's emphasis on, 43; of landowners in the Old Testament, 47; markets and, 106–7; through compassion, 51–52
gleaning laws, 47, 48
globalization, 24–25, 86, 94
global markets, 24–25
gluttony, 16
God: concern for poor by, 43; justice and love of, 28, 70; materialism and, 26–27; plan of salvation by, 45–46; rejection of, 30–31, 38; restoration by, 38; war with Satan, 16, 31–33; as a worker, 36, 42; worship of, 28–29
Golden Rule, 71
gospel, the, 16–18, 31–32
governments: foreign, 24–25; market intervention by, 105–7; programs

of, 107–9; role in charity by, 106–7; role in markets by, 102
greed, 16
growth, 83–87, 85f5.1, 86, 92, 95

healing, 43
historic injustice, 106
Hobbes, Thomas, 79
Holy Spirit: economic wisdom from, 110–12; fruit of, 50; outpouring of, 40, 46, 61, 100; role of, 45
holy war, 16, 31–33
homo economicus, 26–27
honesty, 49
household code, 42–43
households, 51, 56
humanism: Christianity and, 90–91; development of, 76–80; economics and, 79; God and, 77; scholasticism and, 90; secularism of, 90
human nature, 54, 59
human rights, 104. *See also* rights, rights revolution
Hume, David, 79
Huxley, Aldous, 92

idolatry, 99, 101–2, 103, 105–7
image of God, 27–28, 31, 42, 104, 109
income, 51, 84–86, 85f5.1
industrial economy, 48
Industrial Revolution, 84, 96
injustice: as affliction of economy, 31; within Christianity, 93–94; Jesus as prophetic witness against, 41; opposing, 49–50
institutions, 38–39
integrity, 49
interest, monetary, 75

interests, 22–23
international Slave-Industrial Complex, 96
inventions, 88
Israelites, 38
Italy, 73

Japan, 85f5.1
Jesus: conflict of, 41–42; as example, 41; following, 22–23, 32–33; ministry of, 40; new world of, 111–12; purpose of, 60–61; restoration through, 96–97; return of, 32–33, 44; teaching about work by, 41
Job, book of, 16
jobs, 48
John the Baptist, 61
Joseph, 57
justice: within exchange, 69–72; overview of, 49–52; provisions for, 38, 39

kingdom, 41, 42

labor. *See* working
land, 38, 56
land-based economy, 48
Latin America, 85f5.1
law of nature, 73–74
laws, 38–40
lending, 75
Lewis, C. S., 21
limited-access order, 56–58, 59, 90, 91–92
love, 28
lust, 16
Luther, Martin, 17, 77, 88

Machiavelli, Niccolò, 77, 78–79, 88
marketplace, 41
markets, 101–7

marriage, 37
Marx, Karl, 79
material goods, 20, 93
materialism, 26–27, 31
men, 47
mental health, 87
mentorship programs, 48
mercy, 38, 49–52
Middle Ages, 67–69, 73, 74, 89
middle class, 81, 89–90
Middle East, 74
Mill, John Stuart, 79
money, 20, 22, 75
moral commitments, 94
morality, 94, 95, 104–5
moral philosophy, 68
moral virtues, 104
Moses, 57

natural economics, 56–60
natural law, 74
natural order, 87
natural rights, 73–74
natural social order, 53–56
nature, 54
Nelson, Tom, 50–51
New Testament, economic story of, 40–45
new world, 80–81, 83–91, 111–12
North, Douglass, 54–55, 87

Old Testament, economic story of, 35–40
Onesimus, 43
open-access order: benefits of, 91–92; challenges of, 95, 104; characterizations of, 87–88; Christians' role within, 95–96; costs of, 92; emergence of, 90; moral fragmentation of, 109

pagans, 63
parables, 41
Paul, 43, 51
Pentecost, 45–49, 100
Philemon, 43
philosophy, 59–60, 68
Plato, 23, 70
politics, 105–7, 110
poor, the, 38–39, 43, 45, 51
postindustrial economy, 48
poverty: as affliction of economy, 31; consequences of, 93; defined, 92–93; gleaning laws and, 48; God and, 109; persistence of, 92; rates of, 24; reductions to, 86
power, hierarchies of, 72–73
prayer, 21
price, 71–72
The Prince (Machiavelli), 77, 78
procreation, 37
prophets, 39–40
protecting, 28

racism, 93
Rawls, John, 80
Reformation, the, 78, 88, 89, 91
religion, 59–60, 79–80, 88, 91
reputation, 20–21
resources, 19, 20, 21–25
Rhodes, Michael, 26
rich, 61–62
rights, 89–90
rights revolution, 72–76
roles, economic, 57–58
Russia, 25
Ruth, 39, 47

salvation, 45–46
Satan, 16, 31–33, 40, 52

scarce resources, 19
scholasticism, 67–69, 71, 76–77, 90
scientific progress, 79, 90
Scripture, role of, 45
second coming, 22–23, 32–33, 44
secularism, 77–78, 79–80
segregation, 93
selling. See buying and selling
service, 44, 62–63
sexual harassment, 47, 48
sexuality, 26
sin, 32, 37–38, 40, 41, 54, 100
Sister Catherine (book), 68–69
slavery, 39, 43–44, 75, 93
Smith, Adam, 69
social mobility, 57–58
social order, 53–56, 60, 86
social progress, 79
South Africa, 85
specialization, 22–25, 30
spirituality, decline of, 25–27
spiritual warfare, 16, 31–33
stewardship, 27–31, 35, 44–45
suicide, 87
supernatural economics, 60–63

talents, 22–23
Tanzania, 85
technology, 56–57, 86, 88, 94
time, 20, 21
trade-offs, 19–20
trading, 37

Uganda, 85
United States, 85f5.1
universities, 68

vengeance, 42
vocation. See working
voluntary exchange, 101

wealth, 70

Willard, Dallas, 49–50

wisdom, 110–12

women, 47, 48

working: act of, 36–37; curse on, 37–38; early church perspective on, 62; expanding opportunities for, 50; impact of Reformation on, 89; productivity in, 50–51; providing opportunities for, 47; serving through, 62–63; spiritual formation in, 49; teaching of Jesus about, 41

worship, 28–29

worth, 71–72

wrath, 16

Zacchaeus, 42

SCRIPTURE INDEX

Genesis
1   27
1–2   36, 37
1:22   50
1:27–28   35
2:15   27, 28, 35
2:18   29
3:17   37
3:18   37
3:19   37

Exodus
20:9   21, 50
35:30–35   50

Leviticus
19:9–10   39

Deuteronomy
24:19–22   39

Ruth
2   39

2 Chronicles
1:7–12   8

Psalms
90:17   50
127:2   21, 35
128:2   50

Proverbs
12:11–14   50
14:31   39

16:3   50
18:9   50
22:29   50
24:27   50
31:13–31   50

Ecclesiastes
1:1–11   38
3:22   50
5:6   50
9:10   50

Isaiah
60   40

Jeremiah
29:1–7   38

Matthew
11:4–5   43
11:5   61
25:14–30   50
25:40   43
26:53   42
28:16–20   43

Luke
4:18   44
4:18–19   60–61
6:35   43
6:43   49
12:14   42
19:9   42
19:11–27   50

John
5:17   42, 50

Acts
2   52
2:42–47   43

Romans
12:19   42
14:1–15:7   46

1 Corinthians
7:21   43

Galatians
5:22–23   50

Ephesians
4:11–12   44
4:28   50
5:22–6:9   42

Colossians
3:18–4:1   42
3:23–24   50

1 Thessalonians
4:11   50
5:17   21

2 Thessalonians
3:6–8   51

3:10–12   50

1 Timothy
3:1–13   43
5:8   50, 52
6:17   21, 35

2 Timothy
2:6   50

Titus
2:1–10   43

Philemon
8–22   43

Hebrews
10:24   44
10:25   44

1 Peter
1:18   100
2:13–3:7   43

1 John
3:8   40

Revelation
21:3   46
21:24–26   44
22:5   45

RECLAIMING THE CHRISTIAN INTELLECTUAL TRADITION SERIES

For more information, visit **crossway.org**.